RUINED

BY LYNN NOTTAGE

★

★

DRAMATISTS
PLAY SERVICE
INC.

SPECIAL NOTE

Anyone receiving permission to produce RUINED is required to give credit to the Author as sole and exclusive Author of the Play on the title page of all programs distributed in connection with performances of the Play and in all instances in which the title of the Play appears for purposes of advertising, publicizing or otherwise exploiting the Play and/or a production thereof. The name of the Author must appear on a separate line, in which no other name appears, immediately beneath the title and in size of type equal to 50% of the size of the largest, most prominent letter used for the title of the Play. No person, firm or entity may receive credit larger or more prominent than that accorded the Author. The following acknowledgments must appear on the title page in all programs distributed in connection with performances of the Play, and in all advertising and publicity of one-half page or larger, in size of type not less than 25% of the size of the largest, most prominent letter used for the title of Play:

The World Premiere of RUINED was produced by
The Goodman Theatre
Robert Falls, Artistic Director   Roche Schulfer, Executive Producer
and Manhattan Theatre Club
Lynne Meadow, Artistic Director   Barry Grove, Executive Producer

RUINED was commissioned by The Goodman Theatre.

SPECIAL NOTE ON MUSIC

A CD containing the sheet music and recorded music is required for production. The cost is $20.00, plus shipping and handling. The nonprofessional fee for the use of this music is $25.00 per performance.

RUINED received its world premiere at The Goodman Theatre in Chicago, Illinois, on November 8, 2008. It was coproduced by The Goodman Theatre (Robert Falls, Artistic Director; Roche Schulfer, Executive Producer) and Manhattan Theatre Club (Lynne Meadow, Artistic Director; Barry Grove, Executive Producer). It was directed by Kate Whoriskey; the set design was by Derek McLane; the costume design was by Paul Tazewell; the lighting design was by Peter Kaczorowski; the sound design was by Michael Bodeen and Rob Milburn; the original music was by Dominic Kanza with lyrics by Lynn Nottage; the production stage manager was Kimberly Osgood. The cast was as follows:

SALIMA .... Quincy Tyler Bernstine
JOSEPHINE .... Cherise Boothe
JEROME KISEMBE/SOLDIER .... Chris Chalk
MAMA NADI .... Saidah Arrika Ekulona
SIMON/SOLDIER/MINER/
AID WORKER .... William Jackson Harper
FORTUNE/SOLDIER/MINER .... Chiké Johnson
CHRISTIAN .... Russell Gebert Jones
COMMANDER OSEMBENGA/SOLDIER .... Kevin Mambo
MR. HARARI .... Tom Mardirosian
PASCAL/SOLDIER .... Ali Amin Carter
SOPHIE .... Condola Rashad

The Goodman Theatre/Manhattan Theatre Club coproduction of RUINED subsequently opened Off-Broadway in New York City at City Center Stage I on February 10, 2009. The production stage manager was Donald Fried; the assistant stage manager was Alison DeSantis. The cast remained the same, with the exception of:

PASCAL/SOLDIER .... Ron McBee

CHARACTERS

SALIMA

JOSEPHINE

JEROME KISEMBE

MAMA NADI

SIMON

FORTUNE

CHRISTIAN

COMMANDER OSEMBENGA

MR. HARARI

LAURENT

SOPHIE

AID WORKER

SOLDIERS

MINERS

PLACE

A small mining town in the
Democratic Republic of the Congo.

RUINED

ACT ONE

Scene 1

A small mining town. The sounds of the tropical Ituri rain forest. Democratic Republic of the Congo.

A bar with makeshift furniture and a rundown pool table. A lot of effort has gone into making the worn bar cheerful. A stack of plastic washtubs rests in the corner. An old car battery powers the lights and audio system, a covered bird cage conspicuously sits in the corner of the room.

Mama Nadi, early forties, an attractive woman with an arrogant stride and majestic air, watches Christian, early forties, a perpetually cheerful traveling salesman, knock back a Fanta. His good looks have been worn down by hard living on the road. He wears a suit that might have been considered stylish when new, but it's now nearly ten years old and overly loved. He brushes travel dust from his clothing, and takes a generous sip of his soda.

CHRISTIAN. Ah. Cold. The only cold Fanta in twenty-five kilometers. You don't know how good this tastes. *(Mama flashes a warm, flirtatious smile, then pours herself a Primus beer.)*
MAMA. And where the hell have you been?
CHRISTIAN. It was no easy task getting here.
MAMA. I've been expecting you for the last three weeks. How am I supposed do business? No soap, no cigarettes, no condoms. Not

even a half liter of petrol for the generator.

CHRISTIAN. Why are you picking a fight with me already? I didn't create this damn chaos. Nobody, and I'm telling you, nobody could get through on the main road. Every two kilometers a boy with a Kalashnikov and pockets that need filling. Toll, tax, tariff. They invent reasons to lighten your load.

MAMA. Then why does Mr. Harari always manage to get through?

CHRISTIAN. Mr. Harari doesn't bring you things you need, does he? Mr. Harari has interests that supercede his safety. Me, I still hope to have a family one day. *(Christian laughs, heartily.)*

MAMA. And my lipstick?

CHRISTIAN. Your lipstick? Aye! Did you ask me for lipstick?

MAMA. Of course, I did, you idiot!

CHRISTIAN. Look at the way you speak to me, *Chérie. Comment est-ce possible?* You should be happy I made it here in one piece. *(Christian produces a tube of lipstick from his pocket.)* Play nice or I'll give this to Josephine. She knows how to show her appreciation.

MAMA. Yes, but you always take home a little more than you ask for with Josephine. I hope you know how to use a condom. *(Christian laughs.)*

CHRISTIAN. Are you jealous?

MAMA. Leave me alone, you're too predictable. *(Mama turns away, dismissive.)*

CHRISTIAN. Where are you going? Hey, hey what are you doing? *(Teasingly.) Chérie,* I know you wanted me to forget, so you could yell at me, but you won't get the pleasure this time. *(Christian taunts her with the lipstick. Mama resists the urge to smile.)*

MAMA. Oh shut up and give it to me. *(He passes her the lipstick.)* Thank you, Christian.

CHRISTIAN. I didn't hear you —

MAMA. Don't press your luck. And it better be red. *(Mama grabs a sliver of a broken mirror from behind the rough-hewn bar, and grace-fully applies the lipstick.)*

CHRISTIAN. You don't have to say it. I know you want a husband.

MAMA. Like a hole in my head.

CHRISTIAN. *(Reciting.)*
   What, is this love?
   An unexpected wind,
   A fluctuation,
      fronting the coming of a storm.

Resolve, a thorny bush
Blown asunder and swept away
There, *Chérie.* I give you a poem in lieu of the kiss you won't allow me. *(Christian laughs, warmly. Mama puts out a bowl of peanuts.)*
MAMA. Here. I saved you some groundnuts, *Professor.*
CHRISTIAN. That's all you saved for me?
MAMA. Be smart, and I'll show you the door in one second. *(Mama scolds him with her eyes.)*
CHRISTIAN. Ach, ach … why are you wearing my Grandmama's face? *(Christian mocks her expression. Mama laughs and downs her beer.)*
MAMA. You sure you don't want a beer?
CHRISTIAN. You know me better than that, *Chérie,* I haven't had a drop of liquor in four years.
MAMA. *(Teasing.)* It's cold.
CHRISTIAN. Tst! *(Christian cracks open a few peanuts, and playfully pops them into his mouth. The parrot squawks.)* What's there? In the cage?
MAMA. Oh, that, a grey parrot. Old Papa Batunga passed.
CHRISTIAN. When?
MAMA. Last Thursday. No one wanted the damn bird. It complains too much.
CHRISTIAN. *(Amused.)* Yeah, what does it say? *(Christian walks to the birdcage, and peers under the covering.)*
MAMA. Who the hell knows? It speaks pygmy. He … Old Papa was the last of his tribe. That stupid bird was the only thing he had left to talk to.
CHRISTIAN. *(To bird.)* Hello?
MAMA. He believed as long as the words of the forest people were spoken the spirits would stay alive.
CHRISTIAN. For true? *(Christian pokes his finger into the cage. To Mama.)* What are you going to do with him?
MAMA. Sell it. I don't want it. It stinks. *(Christian pokes at the birdcage.)*
CHRISTIAN. *(To bird.)* Hello.
MAMA. Hey, hey don't put your fingers in there.
CHRISTIAN. Look. He likes me. So Mama, you haven't asked me what else I've brought for you? Go see. *(Christian quickly withdraws his finger.)* Ow. Shit. He bit me.
MAMA. Well, you shouldn't be messing with it. *(Mama laughs.)*

CHRISTIAN. Ow, damn it.

MAMA. *(Impatiently.)* Don't be a crybaby, what did you bring me? Well? ... Are you going to keep me guessing?

CHRISTIAN. Go on. Take a peek in the truck. And don't say I don't think about you. *(Mama smiles.)*

MAMA. How many?

CHRISTIAN. Three.

MAMA. Three? But, I can't use three right now. You know that.

CHRISTIAN. Of course you can. And I'll give you a good price if you take all of them. *(Mama goes to the doorway, and peers out at the offerings, unimpressed.)*

MAMA. I don't know. They look used. Worn.

CHRISTIAN. C'mon, Mama. Take another look. A full look. You've said it yourself business is good. *(Mama considers, then finally.)*

MAMA. Okay, one. That one in front. *(Points into the distance.)*

CHRISTIAN. Three. C'mon, don't make me travel back with them.

MAMA. Just one. How much?

CHRISTIAN. Do you know how difficult it was getting here? The road was completely washed out —

MAMA. All right, all right. I don't need the whole damn saga. Just tell me, how much for the one?

CHRISTIAN. The same as usual plus twenty-five, because ... because ... You understand it wasn't easy to get here with the —

MAMA. I'll give you fifteen.

CHRISTIAN. Ahh! Fifteen? No. That's nothing. Twenty-two. C'mon.

MAMA. Twenty. My best offer. *(Christian mulls it over. He's reluctant.)*

CHRISTIAN. Aye. Okay. Okay. Damn it. Yes. Yes. But I expect another cold Fanta. One from the bottom this time. *(Christian, defeated, exits. Mama smiles victoriously, and retrieves another soda from the refrigerator. She reapplies lipstick for good measure, then counts out her money. Christian reenters proudly bearing two cartons of Ugandan cigarettes. A moment later two women in ragged clothing step tentatively into the bar: Sophie, a luminous beauty with an air of defiance, and Salima, a sturdy peasant woman whose face betrays a world weariness. They hold hands. Mama studies the women, then —)*

MAMA. I said one. That one. *(She points to Sophie.)*

CHRISTIAN. It's been a good week, and I'll tell you what, I'll give you two for the price of one. Why not?

MAMA. Are you deaf? No. Tst! I don't need two more mouths to feed and pester me. *(Mama continues to examine each woman.)*

CHRISTIAN. Take both. Feed them as one. Please, Mama, I'll throw in the cigarettes for cost.

MAMA. But, I'll only pay for one.

CHRISTIAN. Of course. We agree, why are we arguing?

MAMA. *(Yelling.)* Josephine! Josephine! Where is that stupid woman? *(Josephine, a sexy woman in a short Western-style miniskirt and high heels, appears in the beaded doorway. She surveys the new women with obvious contempt.)* Take them out back. Get them washed and some proper clothing.

JOSEPHINE. *Njoo.* [Come.] *(Beat.)* *Sasa.* [Quick.] *(Josephine beckons to the women. They reluctantly follow.)*

MAMA. Wait. *(Mama gestures to Salima, who clings to Sophie.)* You. Come here. *(Salima doesn't move.)* Come. *(Salima clings to Sophie, then slowly walks toward Mama.)* What's your name?

SALIMA. *(Whispers.)* Salima.

MAMA. What?

SALIMA. Salima. *(Mama examines Salima's rough hands.)*

MAMA. Rough. *(With disdain.)* A digger. We'll have to do something about that. *(Salima yanks her hand away. Mama registers the bold gesture.)* And you, come. You're a pretty thing, what's your name?

SOPHIE. *(Gently.)* Sophie.

MAMA. Do you have a smile?

SOPHIE. Yes.

MAMA. Then let me see it. *(Sophie struggles to find a defiant smile.)* Good. Go get washed up. *(A moment.)*

JOSEPHINE. *(Snaps.)* C'mon, now! *(Salima looks to Sophie. She follows. The women follow behind Josephine. Sophie walks with some pain.)*

MAMA. Did you at least tell them this time?

CHRISTIAN. Yes. They know and they came willingly.

MAMA. And — ?

CHRISTIAN. Salima is from a tiny village. No place really. She was captured by rebel soldiers, Mayi-mayi; the poor thing spent nearly five months in the bush as their concubine.

MAMA. And what of her people?

CHRISTIAN. She says her husband is a farmer, and from what I understand, her village won't have her back. Because ... But she's a simple girl, she doesn't have much learning, I wouldn't worry about her.

MAMA. And the other?

9

CHRISTIAN. Sophie. Sophie is …

MAMA. Is what?

CHRISTIAN. … is … ruined. *(A moment.)*

MAMA. *(Enraged.)* You brought me a girl that's ruined?

CHRISTIAN. She cost you nothing.

MAMA. I paid money for her, not the other one. The other one is plain. I have a half a dozen girls like her, I don't need to feed another plain girl.

CHRISTIAN. I know this, okay, don't get worked up. Sophie is a good girl, she won't trouble you.

MAMA. How do I know that?

CHRISTIAN. *(Defensively.)* Because I am telling you. She's seen some very bad times.

MAMA. Yeah? And why is that my concern?

CHRISTIAN. Take her on, just for a month. You'll see she's a good girl. Hard worker. *(Mama gestures toward her genitals.)*

MAMA. But damaged, am I right?

CHRISTIAN. … Yes … Look, militia did ungodly things to the child, took her with … a bayonet and then left her for dead. And she was —

MAMA. *(Snaps.)* I don't need to hear it. Are you done?

CHRISTIAN. *(Passionately.)* Things are gonna get busy, Mama. All along the road people are talking about how this red dirt is rich with Coltan. Suddenly everyone has a shovel, and wants to stake a claim since that boastful pygmy dug up his fortune in the reserve. I guarantee there'll be twice as many miners here by September. And you know all those bastards will be thirsty. So, take her, put her to work for you.

MAMA. And what makes you think I have any use for her?

CHRISTIAN. *(Pleads.)* The girl cooks, cleans, and she sings like an angel. And you … you haven't had nice music here since that one, that beauty Camille got the AIDS.

MAMA. No. A girl like this is bad luck. I can't have it. Josephine! Josephine!

CHRISTIAN. And Mama, she's pretty pretty. She'll keep the miner's eyes happy. I promise.

MAMA. Stop it already, no. You're like a hyena. Won't you shut up, now. *(Josephine enters, put-upon.)*

JOSEPHINE. Yes, Mama.

MAMA. Bring the girl, Sophie, back.

CHRISTIAN. Wait. Give us a minute, Josephine. *(Josephine doesn't move.)* Mama, please. Look, okay, I'm asking you to do me this favor. I've done many things for you over the years. And I don't ask you for a lot in return. Please. The child has no place else to go.

MAMA. I'm sorry, but I'm running a business, not a mission. Take her to the sisters in Bunia, let her weave baskets for them. Josephine, why are you standing there like a fool ... go get the girl.

CHRISTIAN. Wait. *(Josephine addresses both of them.)*

JOSEPHINE. *(Annoyed.)* Do you want me to stay or to go?

MAMA. *(Snaps.)* Get her! *(Josephine sucks her teeth and exits.)*

CHRISTIAN. *(With a tinge of resentment.)* Tst! I remembered your lipstick and everything.

MAMA. Don't look at me that way. I open my doors, and tomorrow I'm refugee camp overrun with suffering. Everyone has their hand open since this damned war began. I can't do it. I keep food in the mouths of eight women, when half the country's starving, so don't give me shit about taking on one more girl.

CHRISTIAN. Look. Have anything you want off of my truck. Anything! I even have some ... some Belgian chocolate.

MAMA. You won't let up. Why are you so damn concerned with this girl? Huh?

CHRISTIAN. C'mon, Mama, please.

MAMA. Chocolate. I always ask you for chocolate, and you always tell me it turns in this heat. How many times have you refused me this year. Huh? But, she must be very very important to you. I see that. Do you want to fuck her or something? *(A moment.)*

CHRISTIAN. She's my sister's only daughter. Okay? I told my family I'd find a place for her ... And here at least I know she'll be safe. Fed. *(He stops himself and gulps down his soda.)* And as you know the village isn't a place for a girl who has been ... ruined. It brings shame, dishonor to the family.

MAMA. *(Ironically.)* But it's okay for her to be here, huh? I'm sorry, but, I can't. I don't have room for another broken girl.

CHRISTIAN. She eats like a bird. Nothing. *(Sophie enters.)*

SOPHIE. Madame.

MAMA. *(Defensively.)* It's Mademoiselle. *(A moment. Mama stares at Sophie, thinking, her resolve slowly softening.)* Come here. *(Sophie walks over to Mama.)* How old are you? *(Sophie meets Mama's eyes.)*

SOPHIE. Eighteen.

MAMA. Yeah? Do you have a beau?

SOPHIE. No. *(Mama's surprised by her haughtiness.)*
MAMA. Are you a student?
SOPHIE. Yes, I was to sit for the university exam.
MAMA. I bet you were good at your studies. Am I right?
SOPHIE. Yes.
MAMA. A *petit* bureaucrat in the making. *(Sophie shifts with discomfort. Her body aches, tears escape her eyes. Mama uses the cloth from her skirt to wipe Sophie's eyes.)* Did they hurt you badly?
SOPHIE. *(Whispered.)* ... Yes.
MAMA. I bet they did. *(Mama studies Sophie. Considers, and then decides.)* Christian, go get me the chocolate.
CHRISTIAN. Does that mean...?
MAMA. I'm doing this for you, 'cuz you've been good to me. *(Whispers to Christian.)* But this is the last time you bring me damaged goods. Understood? It's no good for business.
CHRISTIAN. Thank you. It's the last time. I promise. Thank you.
MAMA. You sing?
SOPHIE. *(Softly.)* Yes.
MAMA. Do you know any popular songs?
SOPHIE. Yes. A few.
CHRISTIAN. Speak up! *(Christian exits.)*
SOPHIE. Yes, Mad — *(Catching herself.)* ... emoiselle.
MAMA. Mama. You do math? Stuff like that?
SOPHIE. Yes, Mama.
MAMA. Good. *(Mama lifts Sophie's chin with her fingers, enviously examining her face.)* Yes, you're very pretty. I can see how that caused you problems. Do you know what kind of place this is?
SOPHIE. Yes, Mama. I think so.
MAMA. Good. *(Mama carefully applies red lipstick to Sophie's mouth.)* Then we have no problems. I expect my girls to be well-behaved and clean. That's all. I provide a bed, food, and clothing. If things are good, everyone gets a little. If things are bad, then Mama eats first. Am I making myself clear? *(Sophie nods.)* Good. Red is your color. *(Sophie doesn't respond.)* Thank you, Mama.
SOPHIE. Thank you, Mama. *(Mama pours a glass of local home-brewed liquor. She holds it out.)*
MAMA. Here. It'll help the pain down below. I know it hurts, because it smells like the rot of meat. So wash good. *(Sophie takes the glass, and slowly drinks the liquor down.)* Don't get too dependent on drink. It'll make you sloppy, and I have no tolerance for sloppiness.

Understood? *(Christian, put-upon, reenters with a faded, but pretty, box of chocolates.)*

CHRISTIAN.   Handmade. Imported. *Très bon.* I hope you're impressed. A Belgian shopkeeper in Bunia ordered them. Real particular. I had a hell of a time trying to find these Goddamn chocolates. And then poof, she's gone. And now I'm stuck with twenty boxes. I tried to pawn them off on Pastor Robbins, but apparently he's on a diet. *(Mama opens the box, surveying the chocolates. She's in seventh heaven. She offers a piece to Sophie, who timidly selects a chocolate.)*

SOPHIE.   *Merci. (Mama bites into the chocolate.)*

MAMA.   Mmm.

CHRISTIAN.   Happy? That's what the good life in Belgium tastes like.

MAMA.   Caramel. *(Savoring.)* Good God, I haven't had caramel in ages. You bastard, you've been holding out on me! Mmm. Smell 'em, the smell reminds me of my mother. She'd take me and my brothers to Kisangani. And she'd buy us each an enormous bag of caramels wrapped in that impossible plastic. You know why? So we wouldn't tell my grandfather about all of the uncles she visited in the big town. She'd sit us on the bank of the river, watching the boats and eating sweaty caramels, while she "visited with uncles." And as long as there were sweets, we didn't breathe a word, not a murmur, to old Papa. *(Sophie eats her chocolate, smiling for the first time. Christian reaches for a chocolate, but Mama quickly slaps his hand and shuts the box.)*

CHRISTIAN.   What about me?

MAMA.   What about you?

CHRISTIAN.   Don't I get one?

MAMA.   No! *(This amuses Sophie. She smiles.)*

CHRISTIAN.   Why are you smiling? You're a lucky girl. You're lucky you have such a good uncle. A lot of men would've left you for dead. *(Sophie's smile disappears.)*

MAMA.   Never mind him. *(To Christian.)* Go, all ready and bring the other stuff in before the vultures steal it!

CHRISTIAN.   Sophie. I'm … you … you be a good girl. Don't make Mama angry.

SOPHIE.   I won't, Uncle. *(Christian exits with apology in his posture. Sophie licks her chocolate-covered fingers as the lights fade.)*

Scene 2

A month later.

The bar. Josephine cranks the generator, and colorful Christmas lights flicker on. The bird cage rests in the back of the bar; periodically the bird makes a raucous.

At the bar, drunk and disheveled rebel soldiers drain their beers and laugh too loudly. Salima, wearing a shiny gold midriff, a colorful traditional wrap, and mismatched yellow heels, shoots pool doing her best to ignore the occasional lustful leers of the soldiers.

Jerome Kisembe, the rebel leader dressed in military uniform, holds court. Mama, toting bowls of peanuts, wears a bright red kerchief around her neck, in recognition of the rebel leaders' colors.

Josephine dirty-dances for Mr. Harari, a handsome tipsy Lebanese mineral merchant sporting a surprisingly pristine safari suit. He is barefoot.

Sophie plows through an upbeat dance song, accompanied by a guitar and drums.

SOPHIE. *(Sings.)*
 The liquid night slowly pours in.
 Languor peels away like a curtain.
 Spirits rise, and tongues loosen
 And the weary ask to be forgiven

 You come here to forget,
 You say drive away all regret.
 And dance like it's the ending
 The ending of the war.

The day's heavy door closes quick
Leaving the scold of the sun behind
Dusk ushers in the forest's music
And your body's free to unwind
(Josephine dances for the men.)

You come here to forget,
You say drive away all regret
And dance like it's the ending
The ending of the war.

But, can the music be all forgiving
Purge the wear and tear of the living?
Will the sound drown out your sorrow,
So you'll remember nothing tomorrow?
(A drunk rebel soldier stands and demands attention.)
REBEL SOLDIER #1. Another! Hey!
MAMA. I hear you! I hear you!
REBEL SOLDIER #1. C'mon! Another! *(He clumsily slams the bottle on the counter, and gestures to Sophie.)* Psst! You! Psst! Psst! *(Another rebel soldier gives Sophie a cat-call. Sophie ignores him. Rebel Soldier #1 turns his attention back to Mama.)* Her! Why won't she come talk to me?
MAMA. You want to talk to her. Behave, and let me see your money. *(Jerome Kisembe, the haughty rebel leader, lets out a roar of a laugh.)*
REBEL SOLDIER #1. The damn beer drained my pocket. It cost too much! You're a fucking thief!
MAMA. Then go somewhere else, and mind your tongue. *(Mama turns away.)*
REBEL SOLDIER #1. Hey. Wait. Wait. I want her to talk to me. Mama, lookie! I have this. *(Rebel Soldier #1 proudly displays a cloth filled with little chunks of ore.)*
MAMA. What is it? Huh? Coltan? Where'd you get it?
REBEL SOLDIER #1. *(Boasting.)* From a miner on the reserve.
MAMA. He just gave it to you?
REBEL SOLDIER #1. *(Snickering.)* Yeah, he give it to me. Dirty poacher been diggin' up our forest, we run 'em off. Run them good, gangsta-style, "muthafucka run!," left 'em for the fucking

15

scavengers. *(Rebel Soldier #1 strikes a hip-hop "gangsta-style" pose. The other rebel soldiers laugh. Mr. Harari, unamused, ever so slightly registers the conversation. Mama laughs.)*

MAMA. Coltan? Let me see. Ah, that's nothing, it's worthless, my friend. A month ago, yes, but now you can't get a handful of meal for it. Too many prospectors. Every miner that walks in here has a bucket of it. Bring me a gram of gold, then we talk.

REBEL SOLDIER #1. What do you mean? Liar! In the city this would fetch me plenty.

MAMA. This ain't the city, is it, soldier? *(He aggressively grabs Mama's wrist.)* This is a nice place for a drink. Yeah? I don't abide by bush laws. If you want to drink like a man, you drink like a man, you want to behave like a gorilla, then go back into the bush. *(The rebel soldiers laugh. He unhands Mama.)*

REBEL SOLDIER #1. C'mon Mama, this is worth plenty! Yeah? *(Again, he gestures to Sophie. He's growing increasingly belligerent.)* Bitch. Why won't she talk to me? *(Frustrated, Rebel Soldier #1 puts the cloth back in his pocket. He broods, silently watching Sophie sway to the music. Then all of sudden he collects himself, and drunkenly makes his way toward her.)* I'll teach her manners! Respect me! *(Rebel Soldier #1 pounds his chest, the other rebel soldier goads him on. Sophie stiffens. Mama quickly steps between them. The musicians stop playing.)*

MAMA. But ... as the Coltan is all you have. I'll take it this time. Now go sit down. Sit down. Please.

REBEL SOLDIER #1. *(Excited.)* Yeah? Now, I want her to talk to me! Will she talk to me?

MAMA. Okay. Okay. Sit. *(Rebel Soldier #1 pulls out the cloth. He gently removes several pieces of the ore.)* Don't be stingy. Tst! Let me see all of it. *(Rebel Soldier #1 reluctantly relinquishes the weathered cloth to Mama. Smiling.)* Salima! Salima, come! *(Salima, disgusted, bristles at the sound of her name. She reluctantly approaches Rebel Soldier #1.)*

REBEL SOLDIER #1. What about her? *(He gestures to Sophie.)*

MAMA. Salima is a better dancer. I promise. Okay. Everyone is happy.

KISEMBE. Soldier, everyone is happy! *(Salima sizes up the drunken Rebel Soldier #1.)*

SALIMA. So, "gangsta," you wanna dance with me? *(She places his arms around her waist. He longingly looks over at Sophie, then pulls Salima close. He leads aggressively.)* Easy.

MAMA. Sophie. *(Sophie, relieved, resumes singing.)*

SOPHIE. *(Sings.)*
> Have another beer, my friend,
> Douse the fire of your fears, my friend,
> Get drunk and foolish on the moment,
> Brush aside the day's heavy judgment
>
> Yes, have another beer, my friend
> Wipe away the angry tears, my friend
> Get drunk and foolish on the moment,
> Brush aside the day's heavy judgment.
>
> 'Cuz, you come here to forget,
> You say drive away all regret.
> And dance like it's the ending
> The ending of the war.
> The ending of the war.
> The ending of the war.

(Applause. Mama, having quenched the fire, fetches her lockbox from a hiding place beneath the counter and puts the ore inside.)

MR. HARARI. That one, she's pretty. *(He gestures to Sophie.)*

JOSEPHINE. *(With disdain.)* Sophie?! She's broken. All of the girls think she's bad luck. *(Josephine leads Mr. Harari to the table, they sit.)*

MR. HARARI. What are you wearing? Where's the dress I bought you?

JOSEPHINE. If I had known you were coming, I'd have put it on.

MR. HARARI. Then what are you waiting for, my darling? *(Josephine exits quickly. Mama, toting her lockbox, joins Mr. Harari at his table.)*

MAMA. What happened to your shoes, Mr. Harari?

MR. HARARI. Your fucking country, some drunk child doing his best impersonation of a rebel soldier liberated my shoes. *(Laughter from pool table.)* Every time I come here I have to buy a new fucking pair of shoes.

MAMA. You're lucky he only wanted your shoes. *Santé. (Cheers. Rebel Soldier #1 gets too friendly with Salima. She lurches away.)*

REBEL SOLDIER #1. Hey!

KISEMBE. Ach, ach, quiet, I'm trying to play here. *(Rebel Soldier #1 grabs Salima onto his lap. Mr. Harari watches the Rebel Soldier #1 and Salima.)*

MR. HARARI. You took that poor man's Coltan. Shame on you.

He probably doesn't know what he gave away for the taste of that woman. *(To Rebel Soldier #1.)* Savor it! The toll to enter that tunnel was very expensive, my friend. *(To Mama.)* We both know how much it would fetch on the market.

MAMA. Six months ago it was just more black dirt. I don't get why everyone's crawling over each other for it.

MR. HARARI. Well, my darling, in this damnable age of the mobile phone it's become quite the precious ore, no? And for whatever reason God has seen fit to bless your backward country with an abundance of it. Now, if that young man had come to me, I would've given him enough money to buy pussy for a month. Even yours. So who's the bigger thief, you or him?

MAMA. He give it to me, you saw. So, does that make me a thief or merely more clever than you. *(Mr. Harari laughs.)*

MR. HARARI. My darling, you'd do well in Kisangani.

MAMA. I do well here, and I'd get homesick in Kisangani. It's a filthy city full of bureaucrats and thieves.

MR. HARARI. Very funny, but I imagine you'd enjoy it, terribly. And I mean that as compliment.

MAMA. Do you have a minute?

MR. HARARI. Of course.

KISEMBE. Soldier! Soldier!

REBEL SOLDIER #2. Chief.

KISEMBE. Bring me my mobile! What're you, an old man? Hurry! *(Mama empties a bag containing a precious stone onto a cloth on the table.)*

MAMA. What do you think? Huh?

MR. HARARI. *(Referring to rough stones.)* Just looking, I can tell you, most of these are worthless. I'm sorry. *(Mama takes out another stone. She discreetly shows it to Mr. Harari.)*

MAMA. What about that one? *(Mr. Harari examines the diamond on the table, then meticulously places a loupe to his eye and examines the stone more closely.)*

MR. HARARI. Hm. It's a rough diamond. Where'd you get this?

MAMA. Don't you worry. I'm holding it for someone. *(Mr. Harari continues to examine the diamond.)*

MR. HARARI. Nice. Yes, you see, there. It carries the light very well.

MAMA. Yeah, yeah, but is it worth anything?

MR. HARARI. … Well —

MAMA. Well —

MR. HARARI. Depends. *(Mama smiles.)* It's raw, and the market —

MAMA. Yeah, yeah but, how much are we talking? A new generator or a plot of land? *(Mr. Harari chuckles.)*

MR. HARARI. Slow down, I can offer you a fairly good price. But, be reasonable, darling, I'm an independent with a family that doesn't appreciate how hard I work. *(Mama takes back the diamond.)*

MAMA. You sound like my old Papa. He was like you, Mr. Harari, work too much, always want more, no rest. He drove his farm hard, too hard. When there was famine our bananas were rotting. He used to say as long as the forest grows a man will never starve.

MR. HARARI. Yes, but does he still have the farm? *(Mama smiles to herself.)*

MAMA. You know better, Mr. Harari, you're in the Congo. Things slip from our fingers like butter. No. When I was eleven, this white man turned up with a piece of paper. It say he have rights to my family land. *(With acid.)* Just like that. Taken! And you want to hear a joke? Poor old Papa bought magic from a friend, he thought a hand full of powder would give him back his land. Everyone talk talk diamonds, but I … I want a powerful slip of paper that says I can cut down forests and dig holes and build to the moon if I choose. I don't want someone to turn up at my door, and take my life from me. Not ever again. But how does a woman get a piece of land, without having to pick up a fucking gun? *(Mr. Harari watches the soldiers.)*

MR. HARARI. I wish I could tell you, but I can't even hold onto a fucking pair of shoes. These idiots keep changing the damn rules. You file papers, and the next day the office is burned down. You buy land, and the next day the Chief's son has built a fucking house on it. I don't know why anybody bothers. Madness. And look now, a hungry pygmy digs a hole in the forest, and suddenly every two-bit militia is battling for the keys to hell.

MAMA. True, but someone must provide them with beer and distractions. *(Mr. Harari laughs. Mama scoops up the diamonds and places them back into her lockbox. Mr. Harari removes the loupe.)*

MR. HARARI. But, be careful; where will I drink if anything happens to you? *(Mr. Harari gives Mama a friendly kiss.)*

MAMA. Don't worry about me. Everything is beautiful. *(Josephine enters proudly sporting an elegant traditional dress. Mr.*

Harari watches Sophie.)
JOSEPHINE. What do you think? *(Mr. Harari shifts his gaze to Josephine.)*
MR. HARARI. Such loveliness. Doesn't she look beautiful?
MAMA. Yes, very. Excuse me. *Karibu.*
MR. HARARI. I just might have to take you home with me.
JOSEPHINE. *(Excited.)* Promise.
MR. HARARI. Of course. *(Josephine hitches up her dress, straddles Mr. Harari, and kisses him.)*
KISEMBE. *(Shouts.)* Mama! Mama!
MAMA. Okay, okay, chief, *sawa sawa.* [okay okay.]
KISEMBE. Two more Primus. And Mama, why can't I get mobile service in this pit?
MAMA. You tell me, you're important, go make it happen!
MR. HARARI. Who's that?
JOSEPHINE. Him? Jerome Kisembe, leader of the rebel militia. He's very powerful. He have sorcerer that give him a charm so he can't be touched by bullet. He's fearless. He is the boss man, the government and the church and anything else he wants to be. *(Harari studies Kisembe.)* Don't look so hard at a man like that. *(Josephine grabs Mr. Harari's face and kisses him. Mama clears the beer bottles from Kisembe's table. The rebel soldier gropes at Salima, then he nips her on the neck.)*
SALIMA. Ow! You jackass. *(Salima pulls away from the rebel soldier and heads for the door. Mama races after her, catching her arm forcefully.)*
MAMA. What's your problem?
SALIMA. Did you see what he did?
MAMA. You selfish girl. Now get back to him. *(Mama shoves Salima toward the rebel soldier. Sophie, watching, walks over to Salima.)*
SOPHIE. Are you all right, Salima?
SALIMA. The dog bit me. *(Whispered.)* I'm not going back over there.
SOPHIE. You have to.
SALIMA. He's filth! It's a man like him that —
SOPHIE. Don't. Mama's looking. *(Tears well up in Salima's eyes.)*
SALIMA. Do you know what he said to me —
SOPHIE. They'll say anything to impress a lady. Half of them are lies. Dirty fucking lies! Go back, don't listen. I'll sing the song you like. *(Sophie gives Salima a kiss on the cheek. Salima's eyes shoot daggers at Mama, and she reluctantly returns to the drunken soldier. Sophie*

launches into. Josephine dirty-dances for Mr. Harari. Sophie sings.)
    Have another beer, my friend
    Wipe away the angry tears, my friend
    Get drunk and foolish on the moment,
    Brush aside the day's heavy judgment.

    'Cuz,
    You come here to forget,
    You say drive away all regret.
    And dance like it's the ending,
    The ending, The ending, The ending,
    And dance like it's the ending.
(Mama watches Salima like a hawk. Lights fade.)

Scene 3

Morning.

Living quarters behind the bar. Ragged wood and straw beds. A poster of a popular African-American pop star hangs over Josephine's bed. Sophie paints Salima's fingernails, as she peruses a worn fashion magazine. Salima shifts in place, agitated.

SALIMA. *(Impatiently.)* C'mon, c'mon, c'mon, Sophie. Finish before she comes back.
SOPHIE. Keep still, will ya. Stop moving. She's with Mr. Harari.
SALIMA. She's gonna kill me if she find out I use her nail polish.
SOPHIE. Well, keep it up, and she's gonna find out one of these days.
SALIMA. But, not today. So hurry! *(Sophie makes a mistake with Salima's nails. Salima yanks her hand away.)* Aye girl, look what you did! *Pumbafu!* [Stupid!]
SOPHIE. What's your problem?!
SALIMA. Nothing. Nothing. I'm fine. *(Salima, frustrated, stands up and walks away.)*
SOPHIE. Yeah? You've been short with me all morning? Don't

turn away. I'm talking to you.

SALIMA. "Smile, Salima. Talk pretty." Them soldiers don't respect nothing. Them miners, they easy, they want drink, company, and it's over. But the soldiers, they want more of you, and —

SOPHIE. Did that man do something to hurt you?

SALIMA. You know what he say? He say fifteen Hema men were shot dead and buried in their own mining pit, in mud so thick it swallow them right into the ground without mercy. He say, one man stuff the Coltan into his mouth to keep the soldiers from stealing his hard work, and they split his belly open with a machete. "It'll show him for stealing," he say, bragging like I should be congratulating him. And then he fucked me, and when he was finished he sat on the floor and wept. He wanted me to hold him. Comfort him.

SOPHIE. And, did you?

SALIMA. No. I'm Hema. One of those men could be my brother.

SOPHIE. Don't even say that. *(Salima is overcome by the possibility.)*

SALIMA. I … I … miss my family. My husband. My baby —

SOPHIE. Stop it! We said we wouldn't talk about it.

SALIMA. Just then I was thinking about Beatrice and how much she liked banana. I feed her like this. I squeeze banana between my fingers and let her suck them, and she'd make a funny little face. Such delight. Delight. *(Emotionally.)* Delight! Delight!

SOPHIE. Shhh! Lower your voice.

SALIMA. Please, let me say my baby's name, Beatrice.

SOPHIE. Shhh!

SALIMA. I wanna go home!

SOPHIE. Now, look at me. Look here, if you leave, where will you go? Huh? Sleep in the bush? Scrounge for food in a stinking refugee camp.

SALIMA. But I wanna — !

SOPHIE. What? Be thrown back out there? Where will you go? Huh? Your husband? Your village? How much goodness did they show you?

SALIMA. *(Wounded.)* Why did you say that?

SOPHIE. I'm sorry, but you know it's true. There is a war going on, and it isn't safe for a woman alone. You know this! It's better this way. Here.

SALIMA. You, you don't have to be with them. Sometimes their hands are so full of rage that it hurts to be touched. This night, I look over at you singing, and you seem almost happy like a sunbird that can fly away if you reach out to touch it.

SOPHIE. Is that what you think? While I'm singing, I'm praying the pain will be gone, but what those men did to me lives inside of my body. Every step I take I feel them in me. Punishing me. And it will be that way for the rest of my life. *(Salima touches Sophie's face.)*

SALIMA. I'm pregnant.

SOPHIE. What?

SALIMA. I'm pregnant. I can't tell Mama. *(Tears fill her eyes. Sophie hugs Salima.)*

SOPHIE. No. Shh. Shh. Okay. Okay. *(Sophie breaks away from Salima.)*

SALIMA. I can't tell Mama, she'll turn me out. *(Sophie digs in a basket for a book.)* What are you doing?

SOPHIE. Shh. Be quiet. I want to show you something. Look, look. *(Sophie pulls money from between the pages of the book.)*

SALIMA. Sophie?!

SOPHIE. Shhh. This is for us. We won't be here forever. Okay.

SALIMA. Where'd you get … the money?

SOPHIE. Don't worry. Mama may be many things, but she don't count so good. And when there's enough we'll get a bus to Bunia. I promise. But you can't say anything, not even to Josephine. Okay?

SALIMA. But if Mama finds out that you're —

SOPHIE. Shhhh. She won't. *(Josephine, bedraggled, enters and throws herself on the bed.)*

JOSEPHINE. What you two whispering about?

SALIMA and SOPHIE. Nothing. *(Sophie hides the nail polish and book beneath the mattress, and places the fashion magazine back on Josephine's bed.)*

JOSEPHINE. God, I'm starving. I thought you were going to save me some fufu.

SOPHIE. I did, I put it on the shelf under the cloth.

SALIMA. I bet that stupid monkey took it again. Pesky creature.

JOSEPHINE. It ain't the monkey, it's Emeline's nasty child. He's a menace. That boy's buttocks would be raw if he were mine. *(Josephine takes off her shirt revealing an enormous disfiguring black scar circumventing her stomach. She tries to hide it. Sophie's eyes are drawn to the scar. To Salima.)* But, if it's you who's been pinching my supper don't think I won't find out. I ain't the only one who's noticed that you getting fat fat off the same food we eating. *(To Sophie.)* What are you looking at? *(A moment.)* No questions. Hang

up my shirt! *Sasa! (Sophie hangs Josephine's shirt on a nail.)*
SALIMA. Tst.
JOSEPHINE. And what's wrong with you?
SALIMA. Nothing. Tst. *(Josephine suspiciously sniffs the air. Then puts on a traditional colorful wrap. A moment. Salima sits back on the bed. Josephine notices her magazine on the bed.)*
JOSEPHINE. Hey, girl, why is my fashion magazine here? Huh?
SALIMA. I ... I had a quick look.
JOSEPHINE. What do you want with it? Can you even read?
SALIMA. Oh shut your mouth, I like looking at the photographs.
JOSEPHINE. Oh c'mon, girl, you've seen them a dozen times. It's the same photographs that were there yesterday.
SALIMA. So why do you care if I look at them?
SOPHIE. *Atsha, makelle.* [Stop the noise.] Let her see it, Josephine. Let's not have the same argument.
JOSEPHINE. There.
SALIMA. *(Whispered.)* Bitch.
JOSEPHINE. What?
SALIMA. Thank you.
JOSEPHINE. Yeah, that's what I thought. *(Josephine tosses the magazine at Salima.)* Girl, I really should charge you for all the times your dirty fingers fuss with it. *(Josephine sucks her teeth.)*
SOPHIE. Oh, give us peace, she doesn't feel well.
JOSEPHINE. No? *(Salima moping, thumbs through the magazine doing her best to ignore Josephine.)*
SALIMA. The only reason I don't read is 'cuz my younger sister get school, and I get good husband.
JOSEPHINE. So where is he?! *(Josephine, ignoring her, turns on the portable radio hanging over her bed.)*
ANNOUNCER. *(Voiceover.) Nous avec reçu des rapports que les bandits armés de Lendu et des groupes rivaux de Hema combattent pour la commande de la ville —*
SALIMA. What's he say?
SOPHIE. Lendu and Hema, fighting near Bunia. *(Josephine quickly turns the radio dial. American R&B music plays. She does a few quick suggestive steps, then lights a cigarette.)*
JOSEPHINE. Hey. Hey. Guess what? Guess what? I'm going to Kisangani next month.
SOPHIE. What?
JOSEPHINE. Mr. Harari is going to take me. Watch out, *Chérie,*

he's promised to set me up in a high-rise apartment. Don't hate, all of this fineness belongs in the city.

SOPHIE. For true?

JOSEPHINE. What, you think I'm lying?

SOPHIE. No, no that's real cool, Josephine. The big town. Yeah, what's it like? Have you been?

JOSEPHINE. Me? ... No. No. *(To Salima.)* And I know you haven't.

SALIMA. How do you know? Huh? I was planning to go sometime next year. My husband —

JOSEPHINE. *(Sarcastically.)* What, he was going to sell his yams in the market?

SALIMA. I'll ask you not to mention my family.

JOSEPHINE. And if I do?

SALIMA. I'm asking you kindly this time. *(Josephine recognizes the weight of her words.)*

JOSEPHINE. I'm tired of hearing about your family. *(Josephine blows smoke at Salima.)*

SALIMA. Mention them again, and I swear to God I'll beat your ass.

JOSEPHINE. Yeah?

SALIMA. Yeah. You don't know what the hell you're talking about.

JOSEPHINE. I don't? All right. Digger! I'm stupid! I don't! You are smarter than all of us. Yeah? That's what you think, huh? *Kiwele wele.* [Dummy.] You wait, girl. I'll forgive you, I will, when you say "Josephine you were so so right."

SOPHIE. Just shut up!

JOSEPHINE. Hey, I'm done. *(Josephine blows a kiss, and throws herself across the bed. Salima, enraged, starts for the door.)*

SOPHIE. Salima, Salima.

JOSEPHINE. *(Taunting.)* Salima! *(Josephine falls on the bed laughing.)*

SOPHIE. What's wrong with you? What did Salima do to you? You make me sick. *(Sophie flicks off the radio.)*

JOSEPHINE. Hey, *jolie fille. (Josephine makes kissing sounds.)*

SOPHIE. Don't talk to me.

JOSEPHINE. I can't talk to you? Who put you on the top shelf? You flutter about here as if God touched only you. What you seem to forget is that this is a whorehouse, *Chérie.*

SOPHIE. Yeah, but, I'm not a whore.

JOSEPHINE. A mere trick of fate. I'm sorry, but let me say what we all know, you are something worse than a whore. So many men have had you that you're worthless. *(A moment. Sophie, wounded,*

25

turns and walks away silently.)
JOSEPHINE. Am I wrong?
SOPHIE. … Yes.
JOSEPHINE. Am I wrong?
SOPHIE. Yes.
JOSEPHINE. My father was chief! *(Sophie heads for the door, Josephine blocks her.)* My father was chief! The most important man in the villages, and when the soldiers raided us, who was kind to me? Huh? Not his second wife. "There she is the chief's daughter!" Or the cowards who pretended not to know me, and did any of them bring a blanket to cover me, did anyone move to help me? NO! So you see, you ain't special! *(Lights fade.)*

Scene 4

Dusk. Generator hums. The bar bustles with activity: miners, prostitutes, and government soldiers. Laughter. Salima and Josephine sit at a table with two government soldiers. Sophie sings.

SOPHIE. *(Sings.)*
   A rare bird on a limb
   sings a song heard by a few.
   A few patient and distant listeners.

   Hear, its sweet call,
   a sound that haunts the forest
   A cry that tells a story,
   harmonious, but time forgotten.

   To be seen, is to be doomed
   It must evade capture,
   And yet the bird
   Still cries out to be heard.

   And yet the bird

26

Still cries out to be heard.

And yet the bird
Still cries out to be heard.
(Mama feeds the parrot.)
MAMA. Hello. Talk to me. You hungry? Yes?
CHRISTIAN. Mama! *(Mama is surprised by Christian, her face lights up.)*
MAMA. Ah, Professor! *(Mama cracks open a couple of sodas. Christian places a box of chocolates and several cartons of cigarettes on the counter. The music stops, and he launches into a poem.)*
CHRISTIAN.

The tidal dance,
a nasty tug of war,
two equally implacable partners
Day fighting night …
And so forth and so on.

Forgive me, I bring you an early poem, but I'm afraid it's running away from my memory. I still hope one day you will hear the music and dance with me.
MAMA. *(Dismissive.)* You're a ridiculous man. *(Mama passes a cold soda to Christian. He blows a kiss to Sophie.)*
CHRISTIAN. Lovely, *Chérie*. It's what I've been waiting for.
MAMA. You're the only man I know who doesn't crave a cold beer at the end of a long drive.
CHRISTIAN. Last time I had a drink, I lost several years of my life. *(Mama hands him a list.)* What's this?
MAMA. A list of everything I know you forgot to bring me. *(Christian examines the list.)*
CHRISTIAN. What? When'd you learn to spell so good?
MAMA. Oh, close your mouth. Sophie wrote it down for me. She's a smart girl, been helping me here and there. *(Christian laughs.)*
CHRISTIAN. You see how things work out. And you, you wanted to turn her away —
MAMA. Are you finished? *(The government soldiers break into loud laughter.)* Those soldiers want a full meal, but never want to pay. Tst. *(The government soldiers laugh. Flirtatiously.)* Professor, I looked out for you on Friday. What the hell happened?
CHRISTIAN. I had to deliver supplies to the mission. Have you heard? Pastor Robbin's been missing for a couple days. *(Sophie and*

a government soldier laugh.) I told them I'd ask about.

MAMA. The white preacher? I'm not surprised. He's got a big fucking mouth. The mission's better off without him, the only thing that old bastard ever did was pass out flaky aspirin and maybe a round of penicillin if you were dying.

CHRISTIAN. Well, the rumor is the pastor's been treating wounded rebel soldiers.

MAMA. *(Concerned.)* Really?

CHRISTIAN. That's what I'm hearing. Things are getting ugly over that way.

MAMA. Since when?

CHRISTIAN. Last week. The militias are battling for control of the area. It is impossible.

MAMA. What about Yaka-Yaka mine? Has the fighting scared off the miners?

CHRISTIAN. I don't know about the miners, but it's scaring me. *(Salima and miner laugh.)* I was just by Yaka-Yaka. When I was there six months ago, it was a forest filled with noisy birds, now it looks like God spooned out heaping mouthfuls of earth! And every stupid bastard is trying to get a taste of it. It's been ugly, *Chérie*, but never like this. Not here.

MAMA. No more talk. *(She's spooked, but doesn't want to show it. She signals for the musicians to play an upbeat song. ["Rare Bird."] The song plays softly. Josephine leads a government soldier to the back.)* There will always be squabbles, ancient and otherwise. Me, I thank God for deep dirty holes like Yaka-Yaka. In my house I try to keep everyone happy.

CHRISTIAN. Don't fool yourself!

MAMA. Hey, hey Professor, are you worried about me? *(Christian gently takes Mama's hand.)*

CHRISTIAN. Of course, *Chérie*. I am a family man at heart. A lover, baby. We could build a nice business together. I have friends in Kampala, I have friends in Bamako, I even have friends in Paris, the city of love. *(Mama laughs, and withdraws her hand away from Christian. His affection throws her off balance.)*

MAMA. You ... are ... a stupid ... man ... with a running tongue. And look here, I have my own business, and I'm not leaving it for a jackass who doesn't have enough sense to buy a new suit.

CHRISTIAN. You are too proud and stubborn, you know that. This is a good suit, *très chic,* so who cares if it's old? And ... don't pretend, *Chérie*, eventually you'll grace me with … a dance.

MAMA. Have a cold beer, it'll flush out some of your foolishness.

CHRISTIAN. Ach, ach, woman! Liquor is not a dance partner I choose. *(Christian does a few seductive dance steps. Just then Commander Osembenga, a pompous peacock of a man in dark sunglasses, a gold chain, and a jogging suit, struts into the bar. He wears a pistol in a harness. Christian nods deferentially. He is accompanied by a government soldier in uniform.)* Monsieur. *(Osembenga stands erect waiting to be acknowledged. Everyone grows silent.)*

MAMA. *(Flirtatiously.)* Good evening.

OSEMBENGA. It is now. *(He gives the place a once-over.)*

MAMA. Can I get you something?

OSEMBENGA. Bring me a cold Primus. A pack of cigarettes, fresh. *(Mama produces a chair for Osembenga, then she fishes into the cooler for a beer.)*

MAMA. *Monsieur,* I must ask you to leave your bullets at the bar, otherwise you don't come in.

OSEMBENGA. And if I choose not to. *(Mama holds the cold beer in her hand.)*

MAMA. Then you don't get served. I don't want any mischief in here. Is that clear? *(Osembenga is charmed by her tenacity. He laughs with the robust authority of a man in charge.)*

OSEMBENGA. Do you know who I am?

MAMA. I'm afraid you must edify me. And then forgive me, if it makes absolutely no difference. Once you step through my door, then you're in my house. And I make the rules here. *(Osembenga laughs again.)*

OSEMBENGA. All right, Mama. Forgive me. *(Osembenga makes a show of removing the bullets from his gun and placing them on the table.)* And who said I don't respect the rule of law? *(Josephine, laughing, runs in from the back. A drunk government soldier chases her. His pants are unzipped.)*

GOVERNMENT SOLDIER #1. Commander, beg my pardon.

OSEMBENGA. Take it easy, young man. Take it easy. We're all off duty. Clean up. We're in Mama's house. *(Osembenga sits down, and unzips his jacket. Mama opens a pack of cigarettes and passes them to Osembenga.)*

MAMA. *Monsieur,* I don't recall seeing you here before.

OSEMBENGA. No. *(Mama lights Osembenga's cigarette.)*

MAMA. What brings you to *mon* hotel?

29

OSEMBENGA. Jerome Kisembe, the rebel leader. *(Osembenga studies her face to gauge the response.)* You know him, of course.

MAMA. I know of him. We all know of him. His name is spoken here at least several times a day. We've felt the sting of his reputation.

OSEMBENGA. So, you do know him.

MAMA. No, as I said I know of him. His men control the road east and the forest to the north of here. *(Osembenga turns his attention to everyone. Scrutiny. Suspicion.)*

OSEMBENGA. Is that so?

MAMA. Yes, but you must know that. *(Osembenga speaks to Mama, but he is clearly addressing everyone.)*

OSEMBENGA. This Jerome Kisembe is a dangerous man. You hide him and his band of renegades in your villages. Give them food, and say you're protecting your liberator. What liberator? What will he give, the people? That is what I want to know? What has he given you, Mama? Hm? A new roof? Food? Peace?

MAMA. Me, I don't need a man to give me anything.

OSEMBENGA. Make a joke, but Kisembe has one goal and that is to make himself rich on your back, Mama. *(Osembenga grows loud and more forthright as he speaks. The bar grows quiet.)* He will burn your crops, steal your women, and make slaves of your men all in the name of peace and reconciliation. Don't believe him. He, and men like him, these careless militias wage a diabolical campaign. They leave stains everywhere they go. And remember the land he claims as his own, it is a national reserve, it is the people's land, our land. And yet he will tell you the government has taken everything, though we're actually paving the way for democracy.

MAMA. I know that, but the government needs to let him know that. But you, I'm only seeing you for the first time. Kisembe I hear his name every day.

OSEMBENGA. Then hear my name, Commander Prestige de Bembe Osembenga, *Banga Liwa.* [Fear death.] *(A moment. Mama absorbs the news, she seems genuinely humbled. Christian retreats to the bar.)* You will hear my name quite a bit from now on.

MAMA. Commander Osembenga, forgive me for not knowing your name. *Karibu.* [Welcome.] It's a pleasure to have such an important man in our company. Allow me to pour you a glass of our very best whiskey. From the U.S of A.

OSEMBENGA. Thank you. A clean glass.

MAMA. Of course. *(Mama fetches Osembenga a glass of whiskey. She makes a show of wiping out the cloudy glass. She pours him a generous glass of whiskey and places the bottle in front of him. Seductively.)* Karibu! We take good care of our visitors. And we offer very good company. Clean company, not like other places. You are safe here. If you need something, anything, while —

OSEMBENGA. You are a practical woman, I know that you have the sense to keep your doors closed to rebel dogs. Am I right?

MAMA. Of course. *(Osembenga gently takes Mama's hand. She allows the intimacy. Christian looks on. Contempt. Jealousy. A miner enters covered in mud.)* Hey, hey my friend. Wash your hands and feet in the bucket outside! *(The miner, annoyed, exits.)* These fucking miners have no respect for nothing. I have to tell that one every time. *(Christian sits at the bar, fuming. Osembenga notices him. Obsequiously.)* Anything you need.

OSEMBENGA. I will keep that in mind. *(Mama politely pulls her hand away from Osembenga. She beckons to Josephine and Salima, who join Osembenga at the table. The government soldiers groan.)*

MAMA. Ladies.

JOSEPHINE. Commander. *(Josephine places her hand on his knee.)*

MAMA. Excuse me a moment. *(Christian grabs Mama's arm as she passes.)*

CHRISTIAN. *(Whispers.)* Watch that one.

MAMA. What? It's always good to have friends in the government, no? *(Mama clears bottles from the government soldiers' tables. The miner reenters, and sits at the bar.)*

GOVERNMENT SOLDIER #1. Another.

MAMA. Show me your money. *(The government soldier holds up his money.)* Sophie! Sophie! What are you standing around for? I'm losing money as I speak. Quick. Quick. Two beers. *(Sophie cracks open two beers, and carries them over to the government soldiers. The government soldier places his money on the table. Sophie picks it up, and quickly slips it into her shirt. She doesn't realize Mama is watching her. The government soldier grabs her onto his lap. Christian protectively rises. Sophie skillfully extracts herself from the government soldier's lap, and exits.)*

CHRISTIAN. Are you okay?

SOPHIE. Yes. *(Christian smiles to himself, and lights a cigarette. A drunken government soldier plops down next to Christian.)*

GOVERNMENT SOLDIER #1. Ça va, Papa?

CHRISTIAN. *Bien merci. (The government soldier stares down*

Christian.)
GOVERNMENT SOLDIER #1. You give me a cigarette, my friend?
CHRISTIAN. *(Nervously.)* Sorry, this is my last one.
GOVERNMENT SOLDIER #1. Yeah? You, buy me cigarette.
CHRISTIAN. What?
GOVERNMENT SOLDIER #1. *(Showing off.)* Buy me cigarette!
CHRISTIAN. Sure. *(Christian reluctantly digs into his pocket, and places money on the counter. Mama places a cigarette on the counter. The government soldier scoops it up triumphantly, and walks away.)* And? Merci? *(The government soldier stops short, and menacingly stares down Christian.)*
OSEMBENGA. Soldier, show this good man the bush hasn't robbed you of your manners. *(A moment.)*
GOVERNMENT SOLDIER #1. Merci. *(Christian acknowledges Commander.)*
OSEMBENGA. Of course. *(The government soldier , embarrassed, angrily drives the miner out of his bar seat. The miner retreats. Christian thankfully acknowledges Osembenga with a nod. Osembenga smiles, and gestures to Mama.)*
MAMA. Yes, Commander.
OSEMBENGA. *(Whispered.)* Who is he?
MAMA. Passing through.
OSEMBENGA. What's his business?
MAMA. Salesmen. He's nobody.
OSEMBENGA. I don't trust him.
MAMA. Does he look dangerous to you?
OSEMBENGA. Everyone looks dangerous to me, until I've shared a drink with them. *(Osembenga sizes up Christian. Deciding.)* Give him a glass of whiskey, and tell him I hope he finds success here. *(Mama pours a glass of whiskey, and walks over to Christian.)*
MAMA. Good news, you've made a friend, the Commander has bought you a drink of whiskey and hopes that you'll find prosperity.
CHRISTIAN. That's very generous, but you know I don't drink. Please, tell him thanks, but no thanks. *(A moment.)*
MAMA. The Commander is buying you a drink. *(Mama places the glass in Christian's hand.)* Raise your glass to him, and smile.
CHRISTIAN. Thank you, but I don't drink.
MAMA. *(Whispered.)* Oh you most certainly do, today. You will drink every last drop of what he offers, and when he buys you

another round you'll drink that as well. You will drink until he decides you've had enough. *(Christian looks over at the smiling Osembenga. He raises his glass to the Osembenga across the room, contemplating the drink for a long hard moment.)*
OSEMBENGA.   Drink up! *(The government soldiers encourage Christian.)*
CHRISTIAN.   I —
MAMA.   Please. *(Whispered.)* He's a very important man. So when he offers you a drink, you drink it.
CHRISTIAN.   Please, Mama.
MAMA.   He can help us, or he can cause us many problems. It's your decision. Remember, if you don't step on the dog's tail, he won't bite you.
OSEMBENGA.   Drink up! *(Nervous, Christian slowly and with difficulty drinks back the liquor, wincing. Osembenga laughs, and signals for Mama to pour him another. She does. The government soldiers cheer Christian on.)* Good. *(Shouts.)* To health and prosperity! *(Christian looks at the second drink. Osembenga encourages him to drink up. Christian nervously knocks back the second shot of whiskey, and winces. Osembenga laughs. The soldiers cheer. Mama pours him another.)*
CHRISTIAN.   Don't make —
MAMA.   Trust me. *(She places the glass in his hand. Christian walks over to Osembenga's table. We aren't sure whether he's going to throw the drink in Osembenga's face or toast him. He forcefully thrusts his drink into the air.)*

Scene 5

Morning. Bar.

Sophie reads from the pages of a romance novel. Josephine and Salima sit listening, rapt.

SOPHIE. *(Reading.)* "The others had left the party, they were alone. She was now painfully aware that there was only the kiss left between them. She felt herself stiffen as he leaned into her. The hairs on her forearms stood on end, and the room suddenly grew several degrees warmer."
JOSEPHINE. Oh, kiss her!
SALIMA. Shh!
SOPHIE. "His lips met hers. She could taste him, smell him, and all at once her body was infused with — " *(Mama enters with the lockbox. Sophie protectively slips the book behind her back. Mama grabs it.)*
MAMA. What's this?
SOPHIE. … A romance, Uncle Christian bought it.
MAMA. A romance?
SOPHIE. Yes. *(Mama examines the book. The women's eyes plead with her not to take it.)*
MAMA. Josephine, we need water in the back, and Salima, the broom is waiting for you in the yard.
SALIMA. Ah Mama, let her finish the chapter.
MAMA. Are you giving me lip? I didn't think so. Come here. Hurry. *(Salima reluctantly walks over to Mama. Mama grabs her wrist and runs her hand over Salima's stomach.)* You must be happy here. You're getting fat fat!
SALIMA. I didn't notice.
MAMA. Well, I have. *(Salima, petrified, isn't sure what Mama's going to do. Then.)* You did good last night.
SALIMA. Thank you. *(Mama tosses the book back to Sophie.)*
JOSEPHINE. You don't care for romance, Mama?
MAMA. Me? No, the problem is I already know how it's going to end. There'll be kissing, fucking, a betrayal, and then the woman will

34

foolishly surrender her heart to an undeserving man. Okay. Move. Move. Ach. Ach. Sophie wait. *(Salima grabs the broom and exits.)*
JOSEPHINE. *(Gesturing to Sophie.)* What about her? How come she never has to fetch water?
MAMA. I need Sophie's help.
JOSEPHINE. Tst!
MAMA. You have a problem with that? You count good? *(Josephine stares down Sophie. Sophie isn't having it. Mama laughs. Salima pokes her head in the door.)*
SALIMA. Mama. Someone's coming around the bend.
MAMA. *(Surprised.)* So early?
JOSEPHINE. Tst! Another stupid miner looking to get his cock wet.
SALIMA. No, I think it's Mr. Harari. *(Josephine runs to the door. Salima smiles, jokingly, at Sophie.)*
JOSEPHINE. What?
SALIMA. "Come with me to the city, my darling."
JOSEPHINE. Don't hate!
SOPHIE. "I'm going to buy you a palace in Lebanon, my darling." *This strikes a nerve. The women laugh.)*
JOSEPHINE. Hey, hey. At least I have somebody, I take care of him good. And he comes back. *(Josephine seductively approaches Sophie. She grabs her close.)* Joke, laugh, *jolie fille,* but we all know a man wants a woman who's complete.
SOPHIE. Okay, stop —
JOSEPHINE. He wants her to open up and allow him to release himself, he wants to pour the whole world into her.
SOPHIE. I said stop!
JOSEPHINE. Can you be that woman?
MAMA. Let her alone. Go get the water!
JOSEPHINE. I was firstborn child! My father was chief!
MAMA. Yeah, and my father was whoever put money in my Mama's pocket! Chief, farmer, who the hell cares? Go! *(A moment. Josephine exits. Salima follows.)* Give Josephine a good smack in the mouth, and she won't bother you no more. *(Mama places the lockbox on the table.)* Here. Count the money from last night. Let me know how we did. *(Sophie opens the lockbox and holds up. Mama skillfully funnels water into the whiskey bottle.)* I don't know where all these men are coming from, but I'm happy for it. *(Sophie pulls out the money, a worn ribbon, and then a small stone.)*
SOPHIE. Why do you keep this pebble?

MAMA. That? It doesn't look like anything. Stupid man, give it to me to hold for a one night of company and four beers not even cold enough to quench his thirst. He said he'd be back for it and he'd pay me. It's a rough diamond. It probably took him a half year of sifting through mud to dig it up, and he promised his simple wife a Chinese motor scooter and fabric from Senegal. And here it is, in my hand, some unfortunate woman's dream. *(Mama places the stone in her lockbox.)*

SOPHIE. What will you do with it? *(Mama chuckles to herself.)*

MAMA. Do? Ha! *(Mama knocks back a shot of watered-down whiskey.)* It still tastes like whiskey. I don't know, but as long as they are foolish enough to give it to me, I'll keep accepting it. My mother taught me that you can follow behind everyone and walk in the dust, or you can walk ahead through the unbroken thorny brush. You may get blood on your ankles, but you arrive first and not covered in the residue of others. This land is fertile and blessed in many regards, and the men are not the only ones entitled to its bounty.

SOPHIE. But what if the man comes back for his stone?

MAMA. A lot of people would sell it, run away. But it is my insurance policy, it is what keeps me from becoming like them. There must always be a part of you that this war can't touch. It'll be here, if he comes back. It's a damn shame, but I keep it for that stupid woman. Too many questions, how'd we do?

SOPHIE. Good. If we —

MAMA. We?

SOPHIE. Charged a little more for the beer, a few more francs, by the end of the year you'll have enough to buy a new generator.

MAMA. Yeah? A new generator? Good. You're quick with numbers. You counted everything from last night?

SOPHIE. Yes.

MAMA. Your tips?

SOPHIE. Yes.

MAMA. Yes? *(A moment. Mama grabs Sophie and reaches into her dress, producing a fold of money.)* Is this yours?

SOPHIE. Yes. I was —

MAMA. So tell me what you're planning to do with my money. *(With edge.)* 'Cuz it's my money.

SOPHIE. I —

MAMA. I, I, I ... what?

SOPHIE. It's not what you think, Mama.

MAMA. "Take her in, give her food." Your uncle begged me. What am I supposed to do? I trust you. Everyone say, she bad luck, but I think this is a smart girl, maybe Mama won't have to do everything by herself. You read books, you speak good like white man — but is this who you want to be?

SOPHIE. I'm sorry, Mama.

MAMA. No. No. I will put you out on your ass. I will let you walk naked down that road, let every scavenger dog have a piece of you, is that what you want? What did you think you were going to do with my money?! *(Mama grabs Sophie and pulls her to the door.)*

SOPHIE. Mama! Please! …

MAMA. You want to be out there? Huh? Huh? Then go! Go! *(Sophie struggles, terrified.)* That's what I thought. *(A beat.)* Now tell me, what were you going to do?

SOPHIE. A woman that come in here said she can help me. She said there is an operation for girls.

MAMA. Don't you lie to me.

SOPHIE. Listen, listen, please listen, they can repair the damage. *(A moment. Mama releases Sophie.)*

MAMA. An operation?

SOPHIE. Yes, he give me this pamphlet. Look, look.

MAMA. And it can make it better?

SOPHIE. Yes. *(Mama puts the money into her lockbox.)*

MAMA. Hm. Congratulations! You're the first girl bold enough to steal from me. *(Laughs.)* Where are your books?

SOPHIE. Under my bed.

MAMA. Go bring them to me. I know you better than you think, girl. *(Lights fade.)*

Scene 6

Bar. Morning light pours in. Josephine struggles with a drunk miner. She finally manages to push him out of the bar, then exits into the back. Salima quickly sneaks food from under the counter. She stuffs fufu into her mouth. The bird sqawks as if to tell on her.

SALIMA. Shh! Shh! *(Christian, winded and on edge, comes rushing into the bar.)* Professor!

CHRISTIAN. Get Mama! *(Salima exits quickly. Christian paces. Mama enters.)*

MAMA. *(She lights up.)* Professor! *(Beat.)* What, what is it?

CHRISTIAN. The white pastor's dead.

MAMA. What? *(Christian sits, then immediately stands.)*

CHRISTIAN. He was dead for over a week before anyone found his body. He was only a hundred meters from the chapel. The cook said it was Osembenga's soldiers. They accused the pastor of aiding rebels. They cut him up beyond recognition. Cut out his eyes and tongue. *(He's nauseated by the notion.)*

MAMA. The pastor? I'm sorry to hear that. *(Mama pours herself a whiskey.)*

CHRISTIAN. Can I have one of those, please?

MAMA. Are you sure?

CHRISTIAN. Just give it to me, damn it! *(Mama hesitantly pours Christian a drink. She stares at him.)* What? *(He gulps it down.)* The policeman said there were no witnesses. No one saw anything, and so there is nothing he can do. Bury him, he said. Me? I barely know the man, and people who worked with him for years were mute, no one knew anything. He was butchered, and no one knows anything.

MAMA. Take it easy.

CHRISTIAN. These ignorant country boys, who wouldn't be able to tell left from right, they put on a uniform and suddenly they're making decisions for us. *Mambo kama hayo siyawezi*, Mama! *Yani hata kidogo! Siyawezi kabisa! Kabisa!* Get me another. [Things like these I can't take, Mama! Not even one bit. I can't, just can't.]

MAMA. The Fantas are cold.

CHRISTIAN. I don't want a Fanta. *(Mama goes behind the counter, and reluctantly pours Christian another drink. His hand slightly quivers as he knocks back the liquor.)* They've killed a white man. Do you know what that means? A missionary. They won't think twice about killing us.

MAMA. A dead pastor is just another dead man, and people here see that every day. I can't think about it right now. I have ten girls to feed, and a business to run. *(Mama buries her face in her palms, overwhelmed.)*

CHRISTIAN. We'll go West where there's no trouble. Between the two of us … The two of us. We'll open a small place. Serve food, drink, dancing. Come with me, Mama. *(Mama isn't convinced. Christian reaches for the bottle of whiskey, Mama snatches it away. Christian slams the bar and goes to a table. Meanwhile two men, Fortune and Simon, silently enter, fatigued and ragged. They carry beat-up rifles and wear dirty, ill-fitting uniforms. Fortune also carries an iron pot. The men are very nervous, which makes Mama uneasy.)*

MAMA. Yes?

FORTUNE. Is this the place of Mama Nadi?

MAMA. Yes, that is me. What can I do for you?

FORTUNE. We'll have a meal and a beer.

MAMA. Okay, no problem. I have fish and fufu from last night.

FORTUNE. Yeah. Good. Good.

MAMA. It ain't hot.

SIMON. We'll have it. *(Mama eyes the men suspiciously. Christian glares at them.)*

MAMA. Please don't be offended, but I'll need to see your money. *(Fortune removes a pile of worn bills from his pocket. The men move to sit.)* Hey. Hey. Hey. Empty your weapons. *(The men hesitate.)*

SIMON. No, our wea —

MAMA. It's the rule. If you want to be fed. *(The men reluctantly remove their clips from their guns and hand them to Mama.)*

FORTUNE. *(To Christian.)* Good morning.

CHRISTIAN. Good morning.

SIMON. Do you have a place for us to wash up?

FORTUNE. In the back maybe. *(A moment.)*

MAMA. *(Suspicious.)* I can bring you a basin of water. *(They sit at the table. Sophie enters. She's surprised to find Christian and Simon.)*

SOPHIE. Uncle.

CHRISTIAN. *Bonjour, mon amour. (She is leery of the men.)*
SOPHIE. What happened to —
CHRISTIAN. Shh. I'm okay. *(Sophie notes the caution in his tone.)*
FORTUNE/SIMON. Good morning. How are you? *(The men politely rise.)*
SOPHIE. Good morning. *(The men sit.)*
MAMA. Bring some water for the basin.
FORTUNE. Please. *(Sophie exits with the basin while Mama serves the beer.)* Thank you.
MAMA. You come from the east?
FORTUNE. No.
MAMA. Farmers?
FORTUNE. NO! We're soldiers! We follow Commander Osembenga! *(Sophie returns with the full basin but Christian signals for her to leave. Christian grows increasingly nervous. He watches the men like a hawk.)*
MAMA. Easy. I don't mean to insult you, soldier. But you look like good men. Men who don't follow trouble. *(Fortune seems reluctant to speak.)*
SIMON. We are —
FORTUNE. I'm told there is a woman here named Salima. Is that true?
CHRISTIAN. There — *(Christian starts to speak, Mama cuts him off.)*
MAMA. Why? Who is looking for her?
FORTUNE. Is she here!? I asked you, is she here!?
MAMA. I'd adjust your tone, Mister.
FORTUNE. Please, I'm looking for a woman named Salima.
MAMA. I have to ask inside. *(Christian and Mama exchange a look.)*
FORTUNE. She's from Kaligili. She has a small scar on her right cheek. Just so.
MAMA. A lot of women come and go. I'll ask around. And may I say who's looking for her?
FORTUNE. Fortune, her husband. *(Christian registers this discovery.)*
MAMA. Excuse me. I'll go ask inside. *(Mama exits. Christian disappears into his drink.)*
SIMON. We'll find her, Fortune. C'mon, Drink up. When was your last cold beer?
FORTUNE. I'm not thirsty. *(Simon drinks.)*
SIMON. Ah, that's nice. It's nice, man. *(Fortune isn't interested.)*

40

FORTUNE. Come on, come on, where is she?

SIMON. Be patient. Man, if she's here we'll find her.

FORTUNE. Why is it taking so long?

SIMON. Take it easy.

FORTUNE. You heard it, the man on the road described Salima. It is her. *(Simon laughs.)* What? *(Fortune paces.)*

SIMON. You say that every time. Maybe it is, maybe it isn't. We've been walking for months, and in every village there is a Salima. You are certain. So please, don't — *(Mama reemerges.)*

MAMA. There is no Salima here.

FORTUNE. *(Shocked.)* What? No! She is here!

MAMA. I'm sorry, you are mistaken. You got bad information.

FORTUNE. Salima! Salima Mukengeshayi!

MAMA. I said she is not here.

FORTUNE. You lying witch! Salima!

MAMA. Call me names, but there's still no Salima here. I think maybe the woman you're looking for is dead.

FORTUNE. She is here! Goddamn you, she is here. *(Fortune flips the table. Mama grabs a machete. Christian brandishes the whiskey bottle like a weapon.)*

MAMA. Please, I said she is not here. And if you insist I will show you how serious I am.

SIMON. We don't want trouble.

MAMA. Now go. Get out! Get the hell out of here.

FORTUNE. Tell Salima, I will be back for her. *(Fortune storms out, Simon follows. The birds raise hell. Christian scolds Mama with her eyes. Blackout.)*

End of Act One

41

ACT TWO

Scene 1

Fortune in his ill-fitting uniform stands outside the bar, like a centurion guarding the gates.

Josephine teases two drunk government soldiers and a miner. Guitar. Drums. Mama and Sophie sing a dance song. Mr. Harari and Christian watch. Festive.

MAMA. *(Sings.)*
  Hey, hey Monsieur.
  Come play, Monsieur,
  Hey, hey Monsieur.
  Come play, Monsieur,
  The Congo sky rages electric,
  As bullets fly like hell's rain,
  Wild flowers wilt, and the forest decays.
  But here we're pouring Champagne.
MAMA and SOPHIE.
  'Cuz a warrior knows no peace,
  When a hungry lion's awake.
  But when that lion's asleep
  The warrior is free to play.
SOPHIE.
  Drape your weariness on my shoulder,
  Sweep travel dust from your heart.
  Villagers die as soldiers grow bolder.
  We party as the world falls apart.
MAMA and SOPHIE.
  'Cuz a warrior knows no peace,
  When a hungry lion's awake.
  But when that lion's asleep

42

The warrior is free to play.
(The drum beats a furious rhythm. Josephine answers with a dance,
which begins playfully, seductively, then slowly becomes increasingly
frenzied. She releases her anger, her pain ... everything. The men cheer
her on, a mob growing louder and more demanding. Josephine desper-
ately grabs at the air as if trying to hold on to something. Her dance
becomes uglier, more frantic. She abruptly stops, overwhelmed. Sophie
goes to her aid.)
MAMA.
    Hey, Monsieur.
    Come play, Monsieur,
    Hey, Monsieur.
    Come play, Monsieur
    The door never closes at Mama's place.
    The door never closes at Mama's place.
(Distant gunfire. The bar grows still. A moment.)
    The door never closes at Mama's place.
(Lights fade.)

Scene 2

Back room. Josephine is asleep.

Salima quickly pulls down her shirt hiding her pregnant
stomach as Mama enters eating a mango.

MAMA. *(To Salima.)* Are you going to hang here in the shadows
until forever? I have a thirsty miner with a good day in his pockets.
SALIMA. Sorry, Mama, but —
MAMA. I need one of you to go make him happy, show him his
hard work isn't for naught. *(Mama clicks her tongue.)* C'mon. C'mon.
SALIMA. *(Whispered.)* But ...
MAMA. Josephine!
JOSEPHINE. Ah! Why is it always me? *(Josephine rises, and exits in*
a huff, as Sophie enters from bathing. Salima nervously looks to the door.)
SALIMA. Is Fortune still outside?

MAMA. Your husband? Yes. He's still standing there, he couldn't be more quiet than if he were a stake driven into the ground. I don't like quiet men.

SALIMA. He's always been so.

MAMA. Well, I wish he wouldn't be "so" outside of my door. *(Salima involuntarily smiles, then ...)*

SALIMA. Why won't he go already? I don't want him to see me.

SOPHIE. He's not leaving until he sees you, Salima. *(Sophie gets dressed.)*

MAMA. Ha. What for? So he can turn his lip up at her again.

SOPHIE. No. C'mon, he's been out there for two nights. If he doesn't love you, why would he still be there.

SALIMA. Yeah?

MAMA. Tst! Both of you are so stupid. He'll see you, love will flood into his eyes, he'll tell you everything you want to hear, and then one morning, I know how it happens, he will begin to ask ugly questions, but he won't be able to hear the answers. And no matter what you say, he won't be satisfied. I know. And *Chérie*, don't look away from me, will you be able to tell him the truth? Huh? We know, don't we? The woman he loved is dead.

SOPHIE. That's not true. He —

MAMA. *(To Salima.)* He left her for dead. *(A moment. Mama's words hit home.)* See. This is your home now. Mama takes care of you. *(Mama takes Salima in her arms.)* But if you want to go back out there, go, but they, your village, your people, they won't understand. Oh, they'll say they will, but they won't. Because, you know, underneath everything, they will be thinking, "She's damaged. She's been had by too many men. She let them, those dirty men, touch her. She's a whore." And Salima, are you strong enough to stomach their hate? It will be worse than anything you've felt yet.

SOPHIE. But he —

MAMA. I'm not being cruel, but your simple life, the one you remember, that ... Yeah the one you're so fond of ... it's vapor, *Chérie.* It's gone. *(Tears flood Salima's eyes.)* Now, uh-uh, don't cry. We keep our faces pretty. I will send him away. Okay? Okay?

SALIMA. Okay.

MAMA. We'll make him go away. Yeah?

SALIMA. Okay. Good.

SOPHIE. No, Mama, please, let her at least talk to him. He wants to take her home.

MAMA. You read too many of those romance novels where every-thing is forgiven with a kiss. Enough, my miner is waiting. So c'mon, one of you! *(Mama suspiciously eyes Salima's belly and exits.)*
SOPHIE. If you don't want to see him, then at least go out there and tell him. He's been sitting outside in the rain for two days, and he's not going to leave.
SALIMA. Let him sit.
SOPHIE. Go, talk to him. Maybe you'll feel differently.
SALIMA. He doesn't know that I'm pregnant. When he sees me, he'll hate me all over again.
SOPHIE. You don't know that. He came all this way. *(A moment.)*
SALIMA. Stupid man. Why did he have to come?
SOPHIE. All you ever talk about is wanting to get away from here. Go with him, Salima. Get the hell out of here! Go!
SALIMA. He called me a filthy dog, and said I tempted them. Why else would it happen? Five months in the bush, passed between the soldiers like a wash rag. Used. I was made poison by their fingers, that is what he said. He had no choice but to turn away from me, because I dishonored him.
SOPHIE. He was hurting. It was sour pride.
SALIMA. Why are you defending him!? Then you go with him!
SOPHIE. I'm not def —
SALIMA. Do you know what I was doing on that morning? I was working in our garden picking the last of the sweet tomatoes. I put Beatrice down in the shade of a frangipani tree, because my back was giving me some trouble. Forgiven? Where was Fortune? He was in town fetching a new iron pot. "Go," I said. "Go, today, man, or you won't have dinner tonight!" I had been after him for a new pot for a month. And finally on that day the damn man had to go and get it. A new pot. The sun was about to crest, but I had to put in another hour before it got too hot. It was such a clear and open sky. This splendid bird, a peacock, had come into the garden to taunt me, and was showing off its feathers. I stooped down and called to the bird. "Wssht, Wssht." And I felt a shadow cut across my back, and when I stood four men were there over me, smiling, wicked schoolboy smiles. "Yes?" I said. And the tall soldier slammed the butt of his gun into my cheek. Just like that. It was so quick, I didn't even know I'd fallen to the ground. Where did they come from? How could I not have heard them?
SOPHIE. You don't have to —

SALIMA. One of the soldiers held me down with his foot. He was so heavy, thick like an ox and his boot was cracked and weathered like it had been left out in the rain for weeks. His boot was pressing my chest and the cracks in the leather had the look of drying sorghum. His foot was so heavy and it was all I could see, as the others ... "took" me. My baby was crying. She was a good baby. Beatrice never cried, but she was crying, screaming. "Shhh," I said. "Shhh." And right then *(Salima closes her eyes.)* A soldier stomped on her head with his boot. And she was quiet. *(A moment. Salima releases.)* Where was everybody? WHERE WAS EVERYBODY? *(Sophie hugs Salima.)*
SOPHIE. It's okay. Take a breath.
SALIMA. I fought them!
SOPHIE. I know.
SALIMA. I did!
SOPHIE. I know.
SALIMA. But they still took me from my home. They took me through the bush, raiding thieves. Fucking demons! "She is for everyone, soup to be had before dinner," that is what someone said. They tied me to a tree by my foot, and the men came whenever they wanted soup. I make fires, I cook food, I listen to their stupid songs, I carry bullets, I clean wounds, I wash blood from their clothing, and, and, and ... I lay there as they tore me to pieces, until I was raw ... five months. Five months. Chained like a goat. These men fighting ... fighting for our liberation. Still I close my eyes and I see such terrible things. Things, I cannot stand to have in my head. How can men be this way? *(A moment.)* It was such a clear and open sky. So, so beautiful. How could I not hear them coming?
SOPHIE. Those men were on a path and we were there. It happened.
SALIMA. A peacock wandered into my garden, and the tomatoes were ripe beyond belief. Our fields of red sorghum were so perfect, it was going to be a fine season. Fortune thought so too, and we could finally think about planning a trip on the ferry to visit his brother. Oh God please give me back that morning. "Forget the pot, Fortune. Stay, ... stay," that's what I would tell him. How did I get in the middle of their fight? What did I do, Sophie? I must have done something.
SOPHIE. You were picking sweet tomatoes. That's all. You didn't do anything wrong. *(Sophie kisses Salima on the cheek.)*
SALIMA. It isn't his baby. It's the child of a monster, and there's

no telling what it will be. Now, he's willing to forgive me, and is it that simple, Sophie? But what happens when the baby is born, will he be able to forgive the child, will I? And, and ... and even if I do, I don't think I'll be able to forgive him.

SOPHIE. You can't know that until you speak to him.

SALIMA. I walked into the family compound expecting wide open arms. An embrace. Five months, suffering. I suffered every single second of it. And my family gave me the back of their heads. And he, the man I loved since I was fourteen, chased me away with a green switch. He beat my ankles raw. And I dishonored him? I dishonored him?! Where was he? Buying a pot? He was too proud to bear my shame ... but not proud enough to protect me from it. Let him sit in the rain.

SOPHIE. Is that really what you want?

SALIMA. Yes.

SOPHIE. He isn't going to leave.

SALIMA. Then I'm sorry for him. *(Lights shift to moonlight.)*

Scene 3

Rain. Moonlight. Outside of the bar.

Fortune stands in the rain. His posture is erect. Music and laughter pours out of the bar. Mama stands seductively in the doorway.

MAMA. The sky doesn't look like it's gonna let up for a long time. My mama used to say, "Careful of the cold rain it carries more men to their death than a storm of arrows."

FORTUNE. Why won't you let me see her?

MAMA. Young man, the woman you're looking for isn't here. But if you want company I have plenty of that. What do you like? *(Seductively.)* I know the challenges of a soldier's life, I hear stories from men every day. And there's nothing better then a gentle hand to pluck out the thorns, and heal the heart. *(Mama runs her hand up her thigh and laughs. Fortune turns away, disgusted. Mama smiles.)*

47

FORTUNE. Please, tell my wife I love her.

MAMA. Yeah. Yeah. I've heard it before. You're not the first man to come here for his wife. But soldier, are you sure this is the place you want to be looking for her?

FORTUNE. Here. Give this to her. *(Fortune lifts an iron pot.)*

MAMA. A pot? *(Mama laughs.)*

FORTUNE. Yes, please. Just give it to her.

MAMA. Very charming. A pot. Is this how you intend to woo a lady? *(Fortune shoves it into her hand. A moment. She refuses the pot.)* You're a nice-looking young man. You seem decent. Go from here. Take care of your land and your mother. *(Two tipsy government soldiers tumble out of the bar.)*

GOVERNMENT SOLDIER #2. Just one more time. One. More. Time.

GOVERNMENT SOLDIER #3. Shut up! That girl doesn't want you.

GOVERNMENT SOLDIER #2. Oh yes, she do. She don't know it, but she do. Let me go.

GOVERNMENT SOLDIER #3. I'm not touching you. *(Drunk, Government Soldier #2 crumples to the ground; the other government soldier finds it hysterically funny.)*

MAMA. *(To Fortune.)* Go home. Have I made myself clear? *(Mama goes into the bar. Fortune fumes.)*

FORTUNE. *(To Government Soldier #3.)* Idiot! Pick him up! God is watching you. *(Government Soldier #3 lifts up his friend, as Simon, out of breath, comes running up to Fortune. Josephine seductively fills the doorway.)*

JOSEPHINE. Ay! Ay! Don't leave me so soon. Where are you going?

SIMON. Fortune! Fortune! *(The two government soldiers disappear into the night.)*

JOSEPHINE. Come back! Let me show you something sweet and pretty. Come. *(Josephine laughs.)*

SIMON. Fortune! *(Simon doubles over, out of breath.)* The Commander is gathering everyone. We march out tomorrow morning. The militia is moving on the next village.

FORTUNE. What about Salima? I can't leave her.

SIMON. But we have our orders. We have to go.

JOSEPHINE. *(Seductively.)* Hello, baby. Come say hello to me. *(His face lights up.)*

SIMON. God help me, look at that sweetness. *(Simon licks his lips. Josephine does several down-and-dirty pelvic thrusts. Fortune tries not to smile.)* Quick. Let me hold some money, so I can go inside and talk to this good time girl. C'mon, C'mon ... C'mon, Fortune. What's your name?

JOSEPHINE. Josephine. Come inside, baby.

FORTUNE. Don't let the witch tempt you.

SIMON. Let's enjoy ourselves, Man, tonight ... At least let me have one more taste of pleasure. A little taste. Just the tip of my tongue. C'mon, man, let me hold some money. *(Simon laughs. Fortune does not respond. Josephine laughs and disappears inside. Fortune silently prays.)* How long are you gonna do this? Huh? We've been up and down the road. It's time to consider that maybe she's dead.

FORTUNE. Then leave! *(A moment. Simon, frustrated, starts to leave, then.)*

SIMON. This makes no sense. You can't stay here, the rebel militia are moving this way And if they find you, they'll kill you. We have to go by morning, with or without her.

FORTUNE. Go!

SIMON. Are you sure? You're becoming like Emmanuel Bwiza whose wife drowned in the river when we were children. Remember, the old fool got drunk on bitterness and lost heself. Look here, Fortune, they're making a joke of you. The men are saying "Why won't the man just take another woman." "Why is he chasing a damaged girl?" *(Fortune impulsively grabs Simon around the neck. The friends struggle. Fortune turns Simon loose.)*

FORTUNE. *(Challenges.)* Say it again!

SIMON. It is not me saying it. It is the other men in the brigade.

FORTUNE. Who?

SIMON. If I tell you, are you going to fight all of them?

FORTUNE. Tell me who!

SIMON. Everyone. Every damn one of them. Okay. *(Fortune releases Simon.)* Man, *Mavi Yako!* [Shit!] It's time to forget her. I'm your cousin, and for three months I've been walking with you, right? Got dirty, got bloody with you. But now, I'm begging you, stop looking. It's time.

FORTUNE. No, I've prayed on this.

SIMON. Come out of the rain. We'll go inside and spend the last of our money, and forget her. C'mon, Fortune. Let's get stupid drunk. Huh? Huh? C'mon. *(Simon tries to drag Fortune into the bar. He resists. Fortune, fuming, raises his fist to Simon.)* If you are angry, then be angry at the men who took her. Think about how they did you, they reached right into your pocket and stole from you. I know Salima since we were children. I love her the same as you. She'd want you to avenge her honor. That is the only way to heal your soul. *(Fortune contemplates his words.)*

FORTUNE. Kill?

SIMON. Yes. *(Fortune laughs ironically.)*

FORTUNE. We are farmers. What are we doing? They tell us shoot and we shoot. But for what are we getting? Salima? A better crop? No, man, we're moving further and further away from home. I want my wife! That's all. I want my family.

SIMON. The Commander gave us orders to kill all deserters.

FORTUNE. Are you going to kill me?

SIMON. I wouldn't have said it a month ago, but I'll say it now. She's gone. *(Simon runs into the darkness. Fortune stands outside of the bar in the pouring rain. Gunfire. A fire fight. The sounds of the forest.)*

Scene 4

The bar.

Christian, drunk and haggard, is in the middle of an energetic story. He stands at the bar nursing a beer. Mr. Harari, Sophie, and Mama stand around listening with urgency.

CHRISTIAN. *(With urgency.)* No, no, no ... listen, listen to me, I've just come from there, and it's true. I saw a boy take a machete to a man, sever his neck, a clean blow and lift the head in the air like a trophy. May God be my witness. Men were hollering. "We strong warriors, we taste victory. We will kill!"

MAMA. Shh, keep it down?!

CHRISTIAN. Oh shit, my hand, my hand is still shaking. This ... this man Osembenga is evil. He plays at democracy. This word we all bandy about. Democracy, and the first opportunity we get, we spit on our neighbors and why? Because he has cattle and I don't. Because he is a fisherman and I am not. But nobody has and nobody will have, except for men like you, Mr. Harari, who have the good sense to come and go, and not give a damn.

MAMA. Oh, hush up.

CHRISTIAN. But we have to pretend that all this ugliness means nothing. We wash the blood off with buckets of frigid water, and whitewash our walls. Our leaders tell us, follow my rules your life will be better, their doctors say take this pill your life will be better, plant these seeds your life will be better, read this book your life will be better, kill your neighbor your life will be better —

MAMA. Stop. Take it outside. You know I don't allow this talk in here. My doors are open to everybody. And that way trouble doesn't settle here.

CHRISTIAN. Well, someone has to say it, otherwise what? We let it go on. Huh?

MAMA. Professor, enough! Stop it now. Leave the philosophizing and preaching to the wretched politicians. I mean it! I won't have it here!

CHRISTIAN. One day it will be at your door, Mama.

MAMA. And then I'll shut it. People come here to leave behind whatever mess they've made out there. That includes you, Professor. *(Two rebel soldiers appear from the back in various stages of undress. Josephine and Jerome Kisembe enter from the back. She buttons his shirt. He pushes her away.)* Sophie, turn on the music. *(Sophie turns on the radio. Congolese hip-hop music plays. Christian attempts to disappear behind his drink. Sophie stands behind the bar drying glasses. Mama walks over to greet the men. The parrot squawks.)* Colonel Kisembe, I hope my girls gave you good company.

KISEMBE. Very. It is good to be back, Mama. Where's everyone?

MAMA. You tell me. It's been this way for a week. I haven't seen but a handful of miners. I bake bread and it goes stale.

KISEMBE. It is Commander Osembenga. He is giving us some trouble.

CHRISTIAN. He's a crazy bastard!

KISEMBE. His men set fire to several of our mining villages, now everyone has fled deeper into the bush.

MAMA. I saw smoke over the trees.

REBEL SOLDIER #3. The mission. They're burning everything

to save bullets. *(Sophie gasps and covers her mouth.)*

KISEMBE. They took machetes to anything that moves. This is their justice. *(Kisembe sits at the table. Josephine spots Mr. Harari and is torn between where to place her affection.)* Believe me, when we find Osembenga and his collaborators, he will be shown the same mercy he showed our people. It's what they deserve. *(To Christian.)* Am I right? Am I right?

CHRISTIAN. *(Reluctantly.)* You are right. But —

KISEMBE. I'm sorry. It's how it has to be. They have done this to us. I see you agree, Mama.

MAMA. Of course. *(Everyone in the bar grows uneasy, afraid of Kisembe's intense erratic energy. They're barely listening to his rhetoric, instead focused on trying not to set him off. Jerome addresses everyone with growing intensity.)*

KISEMBE. They say we are the renegades. We don't respect the rule of law ... but how else do we protect ourselves against their aggression? Huh? How do we feed our families? Ay? They bring soldiers from Uganda, drive us from our land and make us refugees ... and then turn us into criminals when we protest or try to protect ourselves. How can we let the government carve up our most valuable land to serve to companies in China. It's our land. Ask the Mbuti, they can describe every inch of the forest as if were their own flesh. Am I telling the truth?

MAMA. Here's to the truth! *(Kisembe, pleased with his own words, places a cigarette in his mouth. A young rebel soldier quickly lights it for him. Kisembe stares hard at Christian, who averts his gaze, and nervously raises his glass.)*

CHRISTIAN. The truth! *(Mr. Harari uses the awkward silence to interject.)*

MR. HARARI. Has Osembenga shut down production at Yaka-Yaka mine?

KISEMBE. And you are?

MR. HARARI. I'm sorry, Colonel, may I offer you my card? *(Mr. Harari passes Kisembe his card. The rebel leader examines it.)*

KISEMBE. Ha-ra-i?

MR. HARARI. Harari. Yes. Please. Let me buy you a drink. *(Mr. Harari signals Sophie to bring a bottle of whiskey over to Kisembe.)* I handle mostly minerals, some precious stones, but I have contacts for everything. My mobile is always on. *(Sophie pours two glasses.)*

KISEMBE. Thank you. *(Kisembe takes the bottle of whiskey and slips the card into his pocket, by way of dismissing Mr. Harari, who backs away. Mama wraps her arms around Kisembe's shoulders.)*

MAMA. Come, gentlemen. You will be treated like warriors, here. *(Kisembe signals to his men. They follow him toward the door.)*

KISEMBE. I wish we could stay all day, but duty calls.

MAMA. No! So soon? *(Mama signals to Josephine, who refuses to budge, instead sits on Mr. Harari's lap. Mr. Harari tenses.)*

Mr. HARARI. *(Whispers.)* Go!

JOSEPHINE. No. *(Kisembe and his men collect their guns and leave. A moment. Relief. Christian slaps his thigh and stands up. He does a spot-on imitation of the haughty swagger of the rebel leader.)*

CHRISTIAN. Girl. Quick. Quick. Bring me a beer, so I can wash it down with Osembenga's blood. *(Sophie and Josephine laugh. Mr. Harari is too nervous to enjoy the show.)*

SOPHIE. Yes, Colonel.

CHRISTIAN. *(Imitating Kisembe.)* Woman, are you addressing me as Colonel?

SOPHIE. Yes. Colonel.

CHRISTIAN. Don't you know who I am? I am from here on in, to be known as the Great Commander of All Things Wise and Wonderful, with the Heart of a Hundred Lions in Battle.

SOPHIE. I'm so sorry, Great Commander of All Things Wise and —

CHRISTIAN. Wonderful with the Heart of a Hundred Lions in Battle. Don't you forget that! *(Christian does a playful mocking warrior dance. Sophie taps out a rhythm on the counter. The drummer joins in. Mama laughs.)*

MAMA. You are a fool! *(Mama carries empty bottles to the back. Unseen, the formidable Commander Osembenga and a sullen soldier, Laurent, enter. They wear black berets and muddy uniforms. A moment. Christian stops his dance abruptly.)*

OSEMBENGA. Don't stop you. Go on.

CHRISTIAN. Commander Osembenga.

OSEMBENGA. Continue. *(Christian finishes his dance, now drained of its verve and humor. Osembenga smiles, and claps his hands. Christian dances until Osembenga stops clapping, releasing him from the dance. Osembenga acknowledges Mr. Harari with a polite nod. The two soldiers ritualistically empty the bullets from their guns.)* Where is Mama?

SOPHIE. She's in the back. *(Yells.)* Mama! Mama!

53

OSEMBENGA. *(Suspiciously.)* I saw a truck leaving? Whose was it? *(A moment.)*

CHRISTIAN. *(Lying.)* Uh … aid worker.

OSEMBENGA. Oh? Good-looking vehicle. Expensive. Eight cylinders.

CHRISTIAN. Yes.

OSEMBENGA. Sturdy. It looked like it could take the road during rainy season.

CHRISTIAN. Probably. *(Osembenga approves.)*

SOPHIE. Mama!

MAMA. *(Annoyed.)* Why are you calling me?! You know I'm busy. *(Mama stops short when she sees Osembenga. She conjures a warm smile.)* Commander Osembenga. *Karibu.* *(Nervously.)* We … how are you? *(Mama glances at the door.)*

OSEMBENGA. Run ragged, if the truth be told. Two Primus, cold, and a pack of cigarettes. *(Mama directs Sophie to get beers for the men. Osembenga strokes Mama's backside. She playfully swats away his hand.)* You look good today.

MAMA. You should have seen me yesterday.

OSEMBENGA. I wish I had, but I was otherwise engaged.

MAMA. Yeah? We heard you had some trouble. Kisembe.

OSEMBENGA. Is that what is being said? Not trouble! Slight irritation. But you'd be pleased to know, we're close to shutting down Kisembe and his militia. We finally have him on the run. He won't be troubling the people here very much longer.

MAMA. Is that so?

OSEMBENGA. My guess, he's heading east. He'll need to come through here. He can't hide from me. It's the only passable road.

MAMA. I saw smoke over the trees.

OSEMBENGA. That bastard and his cronies attacked the hospital.

MR. HARARI. The hospital? Why?

OSEMBENGA. Because they are imbeciles. I don't know. Looking for medicine. Morphine. Who the hell knows? They rounded up and killed mostly Hema patients. *(To Sophie.)* Tsst. Tsst. You, bring me some groundnuts. *(To Mama.)* It was chaos. When we arrived we found the hospital staff tied by their hands and cut up like meat.

LAURENT. One man's heart was missing. *(Sophie covers her mouth with disgust.)*

MAMA. *(Disgusted.)* What?

OSEMBENGA. And he accuses us of being the barbarians? Don't

worry, I've given my soldiers the liberty to control the situation. And control it they will. I am afraid this is what must be done. They force our hand. *(Osembenga takes sadistic delight in this notion. Sophie cringes as she places beer and peanuts on the table for Osembenga. He grabs Sophie's wrist and pulls her toward him. Laughing.)* Come here, you pretty pretty thing. *(Osembenga aggressively grabs Sophie around the buttocks and pulls her onto his lap. Laughing.)* What? You don't like what I'm wearing? *(Sophie tries to gently pry herself loose. Christian, sensing tension, moves toward them. Laurent intervenes.)* You don't like men in uniforms? You don't like men, maybe. Is that it? *(A moment. Sophie struggles to free herself. Mama, sensing the tension.)*

MAMA. Sophie, come here. Let —

OSEMBENGA. *(Smiling, Osembenga pulls Sophie onto his lap.)* Hey. We are talking. We are talking, yeah? *(Osembenga gently runs his hand up her leg.)* Jolie fille! Je connais pas votre nom. [Pretty girl! I do not know your name.] *(Sophie tenses. Osembenga moves his hand up her skirt. Sophie gasps and struggles harder.)*

SOPHIE. *(Hisses.)* Let go of me! *(Sophie pushes away, shocked, from Osembenga. Christian rushes in to protect her, as Osembenga lunges for her. Mama blocks him. Laurent rushes to aid Osembenga.)*

MAMA. Sophie, shush! Enough. Commander, ignore her, there are other girls for you. Come. Come.

OSEMBENGA. Bring this girl around back, my men will teach her a lesson. She needs proper schooling. *(Laurent shoves Christian out of the way and grabs Sophie. This is the first time we've seen Mama scared. Sophie spits on Osembenga's feet.)*

MAMA. Sophie. *(Mama, horrified bends down and wipes the spit from Osembenga's shoes. Osembenga glares at Sophie. She shouts as if possessed.)*

SOPHIE. I am dead.

MAMA. No!

SOPHIE. *(Possessed.)* I am dead! *Shetani!* [Satan!] Fuck a corpse! What would that make you? *(Osembenga is thrown. Christian quickly pulls Sophie away.)*

OSEMBENGA. I'm trying to bring order here, and this girl spits on my feet. You see, this is what I have to deal with. This is the problem.

MAMA. Gentlemen, Commander, this is not our way … we want you to be comfortable and happy here, let me show you the pleasures of Mama Nadi's. *(A moment. A standoff.)*

OSEMBENGA. Then Mama you show me. (*Osembenga checks his anger. He smiles, and blows a kiss at Sophie. He takes Mama's arm, and pulls her to the back with his man. Sophie desperately scrubs her hands in the basin. Mr. Harari pours himself a healthy drink.*)

MR. HARARI. Okay. Let's not overreact. Everything's going to be fine.

CHRISTIAN. (*Whispers.*) Sophie, are you crazy? What are doing? (*Josephine stops Sophie, who is scrubbing her hands raw.*)

JOSEPHINE. Stop it. Stop it. (*Josephine hugs Sophie tightly.*) Shh. Shhh. (*Mama furiously enters. She slaps Sophie across the face.*)

MAMA. (*Enraged.*) Next time I will put you out for the vultures. I don't care if that was the man who slit your mother's throat. Do you understand me? You could have gotten all of us killed. What do you have to say to me?

SOPHIE. … Sorry, Mama.

MAMA. You're lucky the Commander is generous. I had to plead with him to give you another chance. Now you go in there and make sure that his cock is clean. Am I making myself clear?

SOPHIE. Please —

MAMA. Now get outta my sight. (*Mama grabs Sophie and thrusts her into the back. Mr. Harari, Christian and Josephine stare at Mama. A moment. Mama goes behind the bar and pours herself a drink.*) What?

CHRISTIAN. Don't make her do that!

MAMA. What if Osembenga had been more than offended. What then? Who would protect my business, if he turned on me? It is but for the grace of God, that he didn't beat her to the ground. And now I have to give away business to keep him and his filthy soldiers happy.

CHRISTIAN. But if —

MAMA. Not a word from you. You have a problem, then leave.

CHRISTIAN. Business. Just then when you said it, it sounded vulgar, polluted.

MAMA. Are you going to lecture me, Professor? Turn your dirty finger away from me. (*Christian is stung by her words.*)

CHRISTIAN. Mama?

MAMA. What, *Chérie*? (*Mama laughs.*)

CHRISTIAN. (*Wounded.*) Forget it! Bring me another beer. There's my money. (*Christian slams the money down on the counter.*) You understand that, don't you? You like that? There's your fucking money. (*Mama slowly picks up the money and puts it in her apron. She ceremoniously cracks open a beer and places it in front of Christian.*)

MAMA. Drink up, you fucking drunk.

CHRISTIAN. What's wrong with you? *(Christian snatches up his beer and retreats into the corner. He drinks it down quickly.)*

MAMA. You men kill me. You come in here, drink your beer, take your pleasure, and then wanna judge the way I run my "business." The front door swings both ways. I don't force anyone's hand. My girls, ask them, Emilene, Mazima, Josephine, ask them, they'd rather be here, any day, than back out there in their villages where they are taken without regard. They're safer with me, than in their own homes, because this country is picked clean, while men, poets like you, drink beer, eats nuts, and look for someplace to disappear. And I am without mercy, is that what you're saying? Because I give them something other than a beggar's cup. *(With ferocity.)* I didn't come to this place as Mama Nadi, I found her the same way miners find their wealth in the muck. I stumbled off of that road without two twigs to start a fire. I turned a basket of sweets and soggy biscuits into a business. I don't give a damn what any of you think. This is my place, Mama Nadi's. *(Christian begins to exit.)* Of course. *(Mama's words stop him. He walks up to Mama.)*

CHRISTIAN.

The black rope of water
 towing
a rusted ferry
fighting the current of time
an insatiable flow,
Drifting, without enough kerosene to get
through the dark nights.
The destination
always a port away

MAMA. *(She spits.)* It's wind. If you can't place it on a scale, it's nothing. *(Christian heads for the door.)* You'll be back when you need another beer.

CHRISTIAN. I don't think so. *(Christian absorbs the blow, then storms outside in a huff. Josephine leads Mr. Harari to the back. Mama is left alone onstage to weigh the enormity of what she has done. Lights fade.)*

Scene 5

Outside of the bar.

Osembenga and Laurent stumble out of Mama Nadi's place, laughing.

OSEMBENGA. I always like the taste of something new.

FORTUNE. Commander! Commander!

OSEMBENGA. Yes?

FORTUNE. I'm sorry to disturb you, but I ...

OSEMBENGA. Yes?

FORTUNE. I saw Jerome Kisembe.

OSEMBENGA. Who are you?

FORTUNE. I am Fortune Mukengeshayi, I'm with your brigade.

OSEMBENGA. Jerome Kisembe?

FORTUNE. Yes ... He was inside Mama Nadi's.

OSEMBENGA. Inside here?

FORTUNE. Yes, I saw him. She was hiding him. I heard him say the rebels are heading south along this road. He will join them tomorrow.

OSEMBENGA. Mama Nadi's?! Here?!

FORTUNE. He just drove south in a white truck! Please, she is holding my wife. I just want to get her back.

OSEMBENGA. *(To Laurent.)* Quick, quick. We'll go after him. Call ahead, prepare the brigade to move out. I'll deal with Mama later! *(They exit with haste.)*

Scene 6

The bar. Dawn.

Morning light pours into the bar. Mr. Harari paces. His traveling bag is perched near the door. Mama enters, catching him off guard.

MAMA. Would you like a drink while you wait? *(Artillery fire, closer than expected.)*
MR. HARARI. Yes. Thank you. A little palm wine. *(Mama settles her nerves, and pours them both a palm wine.)*
MAMA. It's raining hard, you might wanna wait until —
MR. HARARI. I can't. Thank goodness, I found a lift with one of the aid workers. My driver, fucking idiot, took off last night. *(Jokes.)* Apparently he doesn't care for the sound of gunfire.
MAMA. I told you, you didn't pay him enough.
MR. HARARI. This fucking war, *ya Allah ya azim.* It's everybody's and nobody's.
MAMA. Tst!
MR. HARARI. It keeps fracturing and redefining itself, militias form overnight and suddenly a drunken foot-soldier with a tribal vendetta is a rebel leader and in possession of half of the enriched land, but you can't reason with him, because he's only thinking as far as his next drink.
MAMA. Yes, and what is new?
MR. HARARI. The man I shake hands with in the morning is my enemy by sundown, and why? His whims. Because?! His witch doctor says I'm the enemy. I don't know whose hand to grease other than the one directly in front of me. At least I understood Mobutu's brand of chaos. Now, I'm a relative beginner, I must relearn the terms every few months, and make new friends, but who? It's difficult to say, so I must befriend everybody and nobody. And it's utterly exhausting.
MAMA. Let all the mother-hating soldiers fight it out. 'Cuz in the end do you think that will change anything here?

59

MR. HARARI. God only knows. The main road is crowded with folks heading east. There is no shame in leaving, Mama. Part of being in business is knowing when to cut your loses and get out.

MAMA. I have the only pool table in fifty kilometers. Where will people drink if anything happens to me?

MR. HARARI. Eventually you must fly your colors. Take a side. *(Mr. Harari knocks back his drink, and heads for the door looking out for his ride.)*

MAMA. He pays me in gold, he pays me in Coltan. What is worth more? You tell me. What is their argument? I don't know. Who will win? Who cares? There's an old proverb: "Two hungry birds fight over a kernel, just then a third one swoops down and carries it off. Whoops!"

MR. HARARI. You are the most devilish of optimists. You, I don't worry so much about you. But what about a lovely girl like Sophie? *(His words weigh heavily on Mama. Mr. Harari knocks back his drink, and heads for the door looking out for his ride.)* Until next time! *(Distant gunfire. Mr. Harari anxiously goes to the doorway. Mama goes to the bar; she appears conflicted. An internal battle.)*

MAMA. Ah … One thing, Mr. Harari, before you leave can I ask you a favor.

MR. HARARI. Of course. *(Mama opens the lockbox, and carefully lays out the diamond.)*

MAMA. This. *(Mr. Harari's eyes light up.)*

MR. HARARI. Ah. Your insurance policy.

MAMA. *(With irony.)* Yes. My house, my garden to dig in, and a chief's fortune of cows.

MR. HARARI. You are ready to sell?

MAMA. Yes. Take this. *(Hands him the pamphlet.)* It has the name of a man in Bunia, a doctor. He won't trouble you with questions. Use my name.

MR. HARARI. Slow, slow, what do you want me —

MAMA. Just listen. I want you to take her to —

MR. HARARI. *(Confused.)* Josephine? *(Genuinely surprised.)* Be realistic, how would a girl like Josephine survive in the city.

MAMA. No, listen.

MR. HARARI. I can't. She is a country thing, not refined at all.

MAMA. No, listen … I'm talking about Sophie. This will raise enough money for an operation, and whatever she needs to get settled.

MR. HARARI. Sophie?

MAMA. Yes.

MR. HARARI. Why? Operation? What?

MAMA. It's a long conversation, and there isn't time.

MR. HARARI. This is more than —

MAMA. Enough for a life. I know.

MR. HARARI. Are you sure? This diamond will fetch a fairly decent price, you can settle over the border in Uganda. Start fresh.

MAMA. I have ten girls here. What will I do with them? Is there enough room for all of us in the car. No. I can't go. Since I was young, people have found reasons to push me out of my home, men have laid claim to my possessions, but I am not running now. This is my place. Mama Nadi's.

MR. HARARI. But I'm not —

MAMA. You do this for me. I don't want the other women to know. So let's do this quickly.

MR. HARARI. And the doctor's name is on the paper. I'm to call when I get there.

MAMA. Yes. And you give Sophie the money. The money for the stone. Understand. Promise me. It's important. All of it.

MR. HARARI. ... Yes. Are you sure?

MAMA. ... Yes. *(Mama reluctantly passes the diamonds to Mr. Harari.)* Thank you. I'll get her. *(Mama exits. Mr. Harari examines the diamonds with absolute delight. An aid worker comes rushing in.)*

AID WORKER. I'm loaded. We have to go now! Now! Three vehicles are coming in fast. We can't be here.

MR. HARARI. But ... What about —

AID WORKER. *(Panicked.)* Now! I can't wait. C'mon. C'mon. *(Distant gunfire.)*

MR. HARARI. I have to —

AID WORKER. They'll be okay. Us, men, they'll come after us —

MR. HARARI. *(Calls to.)* One minute. Mama! Mama! Come! Mama! I —

AID WORKER. I hafta go! I can't wait. *(The aid worker doesn't have time to listen, he races out. The engine revs.)*

MR. HARARI. Mama! Mama! *(Mr. Harari seems torn, a moment, then he decides. He places the diamond in his pocket and leaves. Silence. Distant gunfire. Mama enters, frantically pulling Sophie.)*

MAMA. When you get there, he has the money to take care of everything. Settle. Make a good life, you hear.

SOPHIE. Why are you doing this for me?

MAMA. Stop, don't ask me stupid questions, just go. Go! *(She tucks a piece of paper into Sophie's hand.)* This is my cousin's wife, all I have is her address. But a motorbike will take you. You say that I am your friend.

SOPHIE. Thank you, Mama. I —

MAMA. No time. You send word through Mr. Harari. Let me know that everything goes well. Okay. *(Sophie hugs Mama. She exits. Mama, elated, goes to pour herself a celebratory drink. She doesn't see Sophie reenter.)*

SOPHIE. He's gone. *(The stage is flooded with intense light. The sound of chaos, shouting, gunfire grows with intensity. Government soldiers pour in. A siege. A white-hot flash. The generator blows. Streams of natural light pour in to the bar. Fortune, Osembenga, Simon, and government soldiers stand over Sophie and Mama.)*

FORTUNE. He was here! I saw him here! *(Osembenga stands over Mama.)*

OSEMBENGA. This soldier said he saw Jerome Kisembe here.

MAMA. This soldier is liar.

FORTUNE. I swear to you! He was here with two men. The same night you were here, Commander!

MAMA. We are friends. Why would I lie to you? This soldier has been menacing us for days. He's crazy. A liar!

FORTUNE. This woman is the devil! She's a witch! She enchanted my wife.

OSEMBENGA. Again. Where is Kisembe?

MAMA. I don't know. Why would I play these games? Don't you think I know better. He is a simple digger. And me, I wouldn't give him what he wants, so he tells tales. Commander, we are friends. You know me. I am with you. Of course. Come, let me get you some whiskey.

OSEMBENGA. *Funga kinua yaké.* [Shut her mouth.] *(Osembenga signals to his soldiers. They ransack the bar. The parrot squawks. Osembenga calmly sits and watches from a chair. He pours himself a whiskey, lights a cigarette as the men turn the place upside down.)*

MAMA. No! *(Fortune takes pleasure in restraining Mama. A soldier drags Josephine from the back. It is chaos. Frightening. Menacing.)*

OSEMBENGA. This can stop. Tell me where, I can find Kisembe.

MAMA. … I don't know where he is.

OSEMBENGA. *(Points to Josephine.)* Take that one. *(A soldier*

grabs Josephine and bends her over the table poised to violate her. The women scream.)
JOSEPHINE. No! No! Tell him, Mama. He was here.
MAMA. Please! *(Salima enters. A pool of blood forms in the middle of her dress.)*
SALIMA. *(Screams.)* STOP! Stop it!
FORTUNE. Salima!
SALIMA. *(Screams.)* For the love of God, stop this! Haven't you done enough to us? Enough! Enough! *(The soldiers stop abruptly, shocked by Salima's defiant voice.)*
MAMA. What did you do?! *(Fortune violently pushes the soldiers out of the way, and races to Salima.)*
FORTUNE. Salima! Salima!
SALIMA. Fortune. *(Fortune scoops Salima into his arms. Mama breaks away from the soldiers.)*
MAMA. Quick go get some hot water and cloth. Salima look at me. You have to look at me, keep your eyes on me. Don't think of anything else. C'mon look at me. *(Salima smiles triumphantly, she takes Fortune's hand. She turns to Osembenga.)*
SALIMA. *(To soldiers and Osembenga.)* You will not fight your battles on my body anymore. *(Salima collapses to the floor. Fortune cradles Salima in his arms. She dies. Blackout.)*

Scene 7

The sounds of the tropical Ituri rain forest. Bar. The birds quietly chatter.

Sophie methodically sweeps the dirt floor with a thatched broom. Josephine washes the countertop. Mama stands in the doorway anxiously watching the road.

SOPHIE. *(Sings.)*
    Have another beer, my friend,
    Douse the fire of your fears, my friend.
    Get drunk and foolish on the moment,
    Brush aside the day's heavy judgment.
(Excited, Mama spots a passing truck.)

    'Cuz you come here to forget,
    You say drink away all regret,
    And dance like it's the ending.

MAMA. Dust rising.

JOSEPHINE. *(Eagerly.)* Who is it?

MAMA. *(Excited.)* I don't know. Blue helmets heading north. Hello? Hello? *(Mama seductively waves. Nothing. Disappointed, she retreats to the table.)* Damn them. How the hell are we supposed to do business? They're draining our blood.

JOSEPHINE. Hey Sophie, give me a hand. *(Josephine and Sophie pick up the basin of water and exit. Mama buries her face in her hands. Christian enters. He whistles. Mama looks up, doing her best to contain her excitement. Christian brushes the travel dust from his brand-new brown suit.)*

MAMA. Look who it is. The wind could have brought me a paying customer, but instead I get you.

CHRISTIAN. Lovely. I'm glad to see after all these months you haven't lost any of your wonderful charm. You're looking fine as ever.

MAMA. Yeah? I'm making do with nothing. *(Christian smiles.)* Who'd you bribe to get past the road block?

CHRISTIAN. I have my ways, and as it turns out the officer on duty has a fondness for Nigerian soap operas and Belgian chocolates. *(Mama finally smiles.)* I'm surprised to find you're still here.

MAMA. Were you expecting me to disappear into the forest and live off roots with the Mbuti? I'm staying put. The war's on the back of the golddiggers; you follow them, you follow trouble. What are you wearing?

CHRISTIAN. You like?

MAMA. They didn't have your size?

CHRISTIAN. Very funny. *Chérie,* your eyes tell me everything I need to know.

MAMA. Tst!

CHRISTIAN. What you have something in your teeth?

MAMA. Business must be good. Yeah?

CHRISTIAN. No, but a man's got to have at least one smart change of clothing, even in times like these ... I heard what happened. *(A moment.)*

MAMA. *C'est la vie.* Salima was a good girl. *(Sophie enters.)*

SOPHIE. Uncle! *(They exchange a long hug.)*

CHRISTIAN. Sophie, *mon amour.* I have something for you.

SOPHIE. *Un livre?*

CHRISTIAN. ... Yes.

SOPHIE. *Merci. (She rips open the brown paper. She pulls out a handful of magazines and a book. A moment.)*

CHRISTIAN. And this. A letter from your mother. Don't expect too much. *(Sophie, shocked, grabs the letter.)*

SOPHIE. *(Overwhelmed.)* Excuse me.

CHRISTIAN. Go! *(Sophie exits.)*

MAMA. I'm surprised to see you. I thought you were through with me.

CHRISTIAN. I was. I didn't come here to see you.

MAMA. *(Wounded.)* Oh?

CHRISTIAN. And —

MAMA. Yes? *(A moment.)* ... Hello, yes?

CHRISTIAN. *(Hesitantly, but genuinely.)* I ... I debated whether even to come, but damn it, I missed you. *(Mama laughs.)* You have nothing to say to me?

MAMA. Do you really want me to respond to your foolishness?

CHRISTIAN. *(Wounded.)* You are a mean-spirited woman. I don't know why I expect the sun to shine where only mold thrives. *(His frankness catches Mama off guard.)*
MAMA. I don't like your tone.
CHRISTIAN. We have unfinished "business"!
MAMA. Look around, there's no business here. There's nothing left. *(Christian looks around. He looks at Mama, shakes his head and smiles.)*
CHRISTIAN. *(Blurts.)* Then Mama, settle down with me.
MAMA. Go home!
CHRISTIAN. What?!
MAMA. You heard me, go the hell home. I don't wanna hear it. I have too much on my mind for this shit.
CHRISTIAN. That's all you have to say. I looked death in the eye on the river road. A boy nearly took out my liver with a bayonet. I'm serious, I drop and kiss the ground that he was a romantic, and spared me when I told him I was man on a mission. *(Mama cracks open a cold beer.)*
MAMA. It's cold, why can't you be happy with that?
CHRISTIAN. Because, it isn't what I want? Bring me a Fanta, please. *(Mama smiles and gets him a Fanta.)*
MAMA. I'll put on some music.
CHRISTIAN. What's the point, you never dance with me. *(Mama laughs.)*
MAMA. Oh shut up, relax, I'll roast some groundnuts. Huh? *(A moment.)*
CHRISTIAN. Why not us?
MAMA. What would we do, Professor? How would it work? The two of us? Imagine. You'd wander. I'd get impatient. I see how men do. We'd argue, fight, and I'd grow resentful. You'd grow jealous. We know this story. It's tiresome.
CHRISTIAN. You know everything, don't you? And if I said, I'd stay, help you run things. Make a legitimate business. A shop. Fix the door. Hang the mirror. Protect you. Make love to you.
MAMA. Do I look like I need protection?
CHRISTIAN. No, but you look like you need someone to make love to you.
MAMA. Do I, now?
CHRISTIAN. Yes. How long has it been, Mama, since you allowed a man to touch you? Huh? A man like me, who isn't looking through you for a way home.

MAMA. Enough. God. You're getting pathetic.

CHRISTIAN. Maybe. But damn it against my better judgement … I love you.

MAMA. *(With contempt.)* Love. What's the point in all this shit? Love is too fragile a sentiment for out here. Think about what happens to the things we "love." It isn't worth it. Love. It is a poisonous word. It will cost us more than it returns. Don't you think? It'll be an unnecessary burden for people like us. And it'll eventually strangle us!

CHRISTIAN. Do you hear what you're saying?

MAMA. It's the truth. Deal with it!

CHRISTIAN. Hm … Why do I bother. If you can't put it on a scale it is nothing, right?! Pardon me. *(Christian, flustered by her response, walks to the door.)*

MAMA. Where are you going?! *(Mama watches suddenly panicked.)* Hey! You heard me. Don't be a baby. *(Christian stops before exiting.)*

CHRISTIAN. We joke. It's fun. But honestly, I'm worn bare. I've been driving this route a long time and I'm getting to the age where I'd like to sleep in the same bed every night. I need familiar company, food that is predictable, conversation that's too easy. If you don't know what I'm talking about, then I'll go. But, please, I'd like to have the truth … why not us? *(A moment. Mama says nothing. Christian starts to leave, but her words catch him —)*

MAMA. *(With surprising vulnerability.)* I'm ruined. *(Louder.)* I'm ruined. *(He absorbs her words.)*

CHRISTIAN. God, I don't know what those men did to you, but I'm sorry for it. I may be an idiot for saying so, but I think we, and I speak as a man, can do better. *(He goes to comfort her, she pulls away until he's forced to hold her in a tight embrace.)*

MAMA. No! Don't touch me! No! *(She struggles to free herself, eventually succumbing to his heartfelt embrace. He kisses her. Sophie walks in.)*

SOPHIE. Oh, I'm sorry. *(Sophie smiles to herself. Mama pulls away.)*

MAMA. Why are you standing there looking like a lost elephant?

SOPHIE. Sorry, Mama. *(Sophie slips out.)*

MAMA. Don't think this changes anything.

CHRISTIAN. Wait, there.

MAMA. Where are you going? *(Christian straightens his suit.)*

CHRISTIAN. I swear to you, this is the last time I'll ask. *(Recites.)*
   A branch lists to and fro,
   An answer to the insurgent wind,
   A circle dance, grace nearly broken,
   But it ends peacefully, stillness welcome.
(He holds his hand out to Mama. A long moment. Finally, she takes his hand and he pulls her into his arms. They begin to dance. At first she's a bit stiff and resistant, but slowly gives in. Guitar music: "Rare Bird." Sophie pulls Josephine into the doorway. They watch the pair dance, incredulously.)
JOSEPHINE. *(Smiling, whispers.)* Go, Mama.
PARROT. Mama! Primus! Mama! Primus! *(Mama and Christian continue their measured dance. Lights slowly fade.)*

End of Play

PROPERTY LIST

Fanta
Glasses
Primus beers
Lipstick
Sliver of mirror
Bowl of peanuts
Birdcage
Cartons of Ugandan cigarrettes
Liquor (whiskey, palm wine)
Box of chocolates
Cloth filled with ore
Lockbox
Pouch with diamond in it
Loupe
Nail polish
Fashion magazine
Pouch with bills of money in it
Sodas
Pistol
Bullets
Dish rag
Coins
Romance novel
Iron pot
Gun ammo clips
Water basin
Machete
Business card
Red scarf
Yellow scarf
Empty bottles
Pamplet
Broom
Brown paper package containing magazines and books
Letter

SOUND EFFECTS

Distant gunfire
Nearby gunfire/sounds of chaos
Rain
Forest sounds
Parrot squawks
Bird chatter
Engine revving

NEW PLAYS

★ **BENGAL TIGER AT THE BAGHDAD ZOO by Rajiv Joseph.** The lives of two American Marines and an Iraqi translator are forever changed by an encounter with a quick-witted tiger who haunts the streets of war-torn Baghdad. "[A] boldly imagined, harrowing and surprisingly funny drama." —*NY Times.* "Tragic yet darkly comic and highly imaginative." —*CurtainUp.* [5M, 2W] ISBN: 978-0-8222-2565-2

★ **THE PITMEN PAINTERS by Lee Hall, inspired by a book by William Feaver.** Based on the triumphant true story, a group of British miners discover a new way to express themselves and unexpectedly become art-world sensations. "Excitingly ambiguous, in-the-moment theater." —*NY Times.* "Heartfelt, moving and deeply politicized." —*Chicago Tribune.* [5M, 2W] ISBN: 978-0-8222-2507-2

★ **RELATIVELY SPEAKING by Ethan Coen, Elaine May and Woody Allen.** In TALKING CURE, Ethan Coen uncovers the sort of insanity that can only come from family. Elaine May explores the hilarity of passing in GEORGE IS DEAD. In HONEYMOON MOTEL, Woody Allen invites you to the sort of wedding day you won't forget. "Firecracker funny." —*NY Times.* "A rollicking good time." —*New Yorker.* [8M, 7W] ISBN: 978-0-8222-2394-8

★ **SONS OF THE PROPHET by Stephen Karam.** If to live is to suffer, then Joseph Douaihy is more alive than most. With unexplained chronic pain and the fate of his reeling family on his shoulders, Joseph's health, sanity, and insurance premium are on the line. "Explosively funny." —*NY Times.* "At once deep, deft and beautifully made." —*New Yorker.* [5M, 3W] ISBN: 978-0-8222-2597-3

★ **THE MOUNTAINTOP by Katori Hall.** A gripping reimagination of events the night before the assassination of the civil rights leader Dr. Martin Luther King, Jr. "An ominous electricity crackles through the opening moments." —*NY Times.* "[A] thrilling, wild, provocative flight of magical realism." —*Associated Press.* "Crackles with theatricality and a humanity more moving than sainthood." —*NY Newsday.* [1M, 1W] ISBN: 978-0-8222-2603-1

★ **ALL NEW PEOPLE by Zach Braff.** Charlie is 35, heartbroken, and just wants some time away from the rest of the world. Long Beach Island seems to be the perfect escape until his solitude is interrupted by a motley parade of misfits who show up and change his plans. "Consistently and sometimes sensationally funny." —*NY Times.* "A morbidly funny play about the trendy new existential condition of being young, adorable, and miserable." —*Variety.* [2M, 2W] ISBN: 978-0-8222-2562-1

DRAMATISTS PLAY SERVICE, INC.
440 Park Avenue South, New York, NY 10016 212-683-8960 Fax 212-213-1539
postmaster@dramatists.com www.dramatists.com

NEW PLAYS

★ **CLYBOURNE PARK by Bruce Norris.** WINNER OF THE 2011 PULITZER PRIZE AND 2012 TONY AWARD. Act One takes place in 1959 as community leaders try to stop the sale of a home to a black family. Act Two is set in the same house in the present day as the now predominantly African-American neighborhood battles to hold its ground. "Vital, sharp-witted and ferociously smart." –*NY Times.* "A theatrical treasure...Indisputably, uproariously funny." –*Entertainment Weekly.* [4M, 3W] ISBN: 978-0-8222-2697-0

★ **WATER BY THE SPOONFUL by Quiara Alegría Hudes.** WINNER OF THE 2012 PULITZER PRIZE. A Puerto Rican veteran is surrounded by the North Philadelphia demons he tried to escape in the service. "This is a very funny, warm, and yes uplifting play." –*Hartford Courant.* "The play is a combination poem, prayer and app on how to cope in an age of uncertainty, speed and chaos." –*Variety.* [4M, 3W] ISBN: 978-0-8222-2716-8

★ **RED by John Logan.** WINNER OF THE 2010 TONY AWARD. Mark Rothko has just landed the biggest commission in the history of modern art. But when his young assistant, Ken, gains the confidence to challenge him, Rothko faces the agonizing possibility that his crowning achievement could also become his undoing. "Intense and exciting." –*NY Times.* "Smart, eloquent entertainment." –*New Yorker.* [2M] ISBN: 978-0-8222-2483-9

★ **VENUS IN FUR by David Ives.** Thomas, a beleaguered playwright/director, is desperate to find an actress to play Vanda, the female lead in his adaptation of the classic sadomasochistic tale *Venus in Fur.* "Ninety minutes of good, kinky fun." –*NY Times.* "A fast-paced journey into one man's entrapment by a clever, vengeful female." –*Associated Press.* [1M, 1W] ISBN: 978-0-8222-2603-1

★ **OTHER DESERT CITIES by Jon Robin Baitz.** Brooke returns home to Palm Springs after a six-year absence and announces that she is about to publish a memoir dredging up a pivotal and tragic event in the family's history—a wound they don't want reopened. "Leaves you feeling both moved and gratifyingly sated." –*NY Times.* "A genuine pleasure." –*NY Post.* [2M, 3W] ISBN: 978-0-8222-2605-5

★ **TRIBES by Nina Raine.** Billy was born deaf into a hearing family and adapts brilliantly to his family's unconventional ways, but it's not until he meets Sylvia, a young woman on the brink of deafness, that he finally understands what it means to be understood. "A smart, lively play." –*NY Times.* "[A] bright and boldly provocative drama." –*Associated Press.* [3M, 2W] ISBN: 978-0-8222-2751-9

DRAMATISTS PLAY SERVICE, INC.
440 Park Avenue South, New York, NY 10016 212-683-8960 Fax 212-213-1539
postmaster@dramatists.com   www.dramatists.com